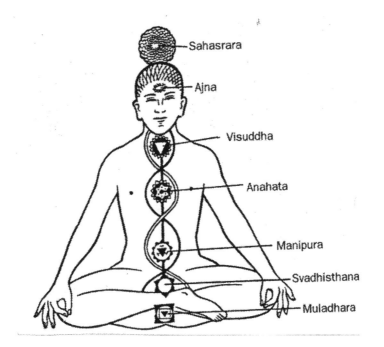

Sahasrara

Ajna

Visuddha

Anahata

Manipura

Svadhisthana

Muladhara

Personal Wellness Through the Old Testament

WILLIAM FAIRBANKS

authorHOUSE

AuthorHouse™
1663 Liberty Drive
Bloomington, IN 47403
www.authorhouse.com
Phone: 1-800-839-8640

First published by AuthorHouse   8/9/2010

ISBN: 978-1-4520-6338-6 (sc)
ISBN: 978-1-4520-6339-3 (e)

Library of Congress Control Number: 2010911886

Printed in the United States of America
Bloomington, Indiana

This book is printed on acid-free paper.

William Fairbanks

Unless otherwise indicated, Bible quotations are taken from the New King James Version Copy right © 1997 by Thomas Nelson, Inc.

Contents

Preface

The Bible, the holy book of Christendom, has been seen in many different ways. It has caused wars, brought peace, comforted some and terrified others. The apostle Paul wrote to his student, Timothy, "All scripture is given by God, and is profitable for doctrine, for reproof, and instruction in righteousness; that the man of God may be perfect, thoroughly furnished unto all good works." Thus the primary purposes of the Bible are to describe the correct way for a person to live, warn of likely deviations from the way, and describe one's optimal journey. It has been seen to a large extent as a historical record of such people as Moses, King David, and the historical Jesus. While this is valid, viewing it in that way misses the main purpose for which it was intended, to aid people in their lives, to make them well and whole.

A profound perspective on the Bible was espoused by a prominent American of a past generation, the psychic, Edgar Cayce. Mr. Cayce did not function in secret as a book on his life, "The Sleeping Prophet", was on the New York Times Bestseller list for some time. His primary contention was that the Bible should be used to benefit mankind physically, mentally, and spiritually. He said that the Old Testament until Abraham was for the benefit of the physical body, and starting with that father of faith, the concern was the mental body. He said that the New Testament was entirely concerned with the spirit. The spiritual body should be looked upon as relationships between more than one person, while the physical and mental bodies are the concern of one individual. By following his teachings, borrowing from other religions such as Buddhism, and using modern tools, such as interpersonal psychology, a unique outlook about wellness for the individual has been arrived at. The primary facet of this methodology is the belief that the Bible is structured in the same way as the human body and mind. When this truth is made manifest it can be realized that the Bible is much like an owner's manual for mankind and it can help make up for deficiencies in the physical and mental aspects of man. While much of this information has been made known by such sources as Edgar Cayce, new discoveries have been made by the author. These discoveries occurred when he noted further correlations between the book and the body.

Much has been said about, and study done concerning the mind-body interface. It is said that the human body can be looked at as an extension of the mind. It is certain that following certain rules can help a person's well-being. This is being emphasized more and more at the start of the 21st century through such disciplines as interpersonal psychology, and it can also be seen historically. Information about the ancient Jews indicates that when they followed the Ten Commandments strictly they were physically and mentally whole, not one feeble person being among them.[1] This was because there was no erroneous behavior whatever among them when they came out of Egypt under Moses as they strictly followed the Ten Commandments and other rules of behavior. This complete adherence to beneficial laws was achieved because if even one of them were broken the perpetrator was eliminated from the population by stoning. There is much to be gained by attempting to follow the owner's manual on how to live in physical and mental well-being.

Another aspect of the Bible which Edgar Cayce pointed out was that the holy book is like the human body to the extent that both are structured in a series of sevens. Mr. Cayce said that the last book of the Bible, Revelation, is a reflection of the first book, Genesis, and both contain many sevens. In this he was espousing a system known in many religions, such as Buddhism, which sees the physical body as related to seven spiritual centers. They are called chakras. There are references to them in sacred writings from cultures all over the world – at widely different places and times and in many writings. The Buddhists, the ancient Chinese, Hindus, Tantric scriptures, Christian mystics, the Kabbala (Jewish), Sufis, Native Americans, and Yogic writings have all described or illustrated these centers of energy. The existence of these centers has been verified by a process known as Kirlian photography which makes them visible on photographic paper.[2]

While the number seven applies to the functioning of bodily systems, the number twelve can also be seen in human processes, specifically those relating to the mind. Psychologists have studied how a person's consciousness is developed over one's lifetime and how the focus of the mind continually varies. The psychologist, Dr. Carol S. Pearson has arrived at a system of twelve elements of mental focus and it will be shown how this system is reflected in the books of the minor prophets.

The findings about common structures in man and the book have a greater impact when it is acknowledged that the Bible has a unique quality in literature, it being inerent. Since it was constructed by fallible humans, there may appear to be minor errors or inconsistencies, and yet the hallmark of scripture is one of inerrancy. This can be verified by a look at the history of its creation. During the reign of Ptolemy II (284-246 B.C.), the first five books of the Hebrew Bible were translated into Greek. The historian, Josephus, inferred that this was a holy process. Ireneus, the Bishop of Lyons in the second century, declared that the fact that there were four Gospels was divinely ordained. Origen, another scholar who had a hand in composing the canon, said, "The Scriptures were composed through the Spirit of God."[3]

Since the Bible is basically inerent and to a large extent organized in the same manner as the human body, it is beneficial to look at scripture as symbolic and not from a historical or literal perspective. Edgar Cayce said in his trace state, "As has been so often given, all places – as Egypt or Sodom or the Crucifixion of the Lord – are conditions, circumstances, experiences, as well as individual places. Then in the minds of those who would attempt or that would seek knowledge, they represent their own experiences. Thus these to the people represent – Egypt, the release from bondage, Gomorrah, as a reckoning with sin –as the Lord was crucified there"[4] Knowing that place names such as Israel, Assyria, and Babylon are symbolic makes it possible to see certain patterns in scripture, and examine oneself so as to make worthwhile attempts at improving one's wellness.

Another aid for seeing helpful system in the Bible is the realization that all numbers in it are sacred. The meaning of a number in the Bible is always the same and these meanings are of real import. The principles involved in this are put forth in "Biblical Mathematics" by Evangelist Ed. F. Vallowe.[5]

These principles concerning scripture may be seen in the writings of a modern prophet, Eckhart Tolle, who wrote in "A New Earth, Awakening to your life's Purpose". He said that this process of personal transformation to a higher form is called enlightenment in the Hindu and Buddhist religions. He said that in the teachings of Jesus it is called salvation. Buddhism teaches that the purpose of enlightenment is to end all suffering something called, "dukkha". In examining how the Old Testament relates to the one who reads it, progress is made through raising one's consciousness by self-examination with ensuing enlightenment. The ancient Jews had a priest atone for their errors with a blood sacrifice once a year on a day called Yom Kippur and the only sin they recognized among themselves was ignorance, the unwillingness to learn. It is certainly true that before purified behavior can be pursued, there must be an increase in information about oneself, something which can be found in abundance in the Old Testament.

Even though information may be found in the Old Testament which can bring such amazing benefits as a cure for cancer, and total mental peacefulness, there will also be a look ahead to the unlimited existence promised in the New Testament. Edgar Cayce said that it was entirely concerned with the spiritual dimension of mankind. Mr. Cayce's primary religious concern can be seen as "Christ consciousness". While he believed in fundamental religious concepts, especially the efficacy of studying the Bible, he felt that all religions, and all creation, was designed for purification of people to make them fit to be members of the universal body of Christ.

Chapter One - The Primary Pattern

A specific way in which wellness may be enhanced through the study of the Old Testament is by seeing a seven-layered structure that is related to both the book and the body. There are seven glands in the physical body which comprise the endocrine system which interface with another body surrounding and in the physical body. This body, which is known as the "aura" has seven primary spiritual centers. After seeing this it will be shown that many areas of the Bible contain a similar seven-fold pattern. The spiritual centers in the body are called, "Chakras" in Sanskrit. They are spinning vortices of energy.

These spiritual centers, are not in the physical body but are in what is known as the ethereal body. A scientific explanation of the ethereal body which contains the seven major chakras is that it is a bio-plasmic body which is like a space suit around the physical body. It has been called the aura because of the many different colors in it. There are four states of matter; solid, liquid, gas, and plasma, and aura is made up of plasma. This plasma which comprises the aura is made up of ions which can be detected by scientific means. .

Until recently information about the aura or bio-plasmic body has been used mainly in eastern religions for meditation. However, in the 1990's knowledge about it has been communicated in the western world. This has occurred at time when eastern meditation has become a common practice and the medical procedure of acupuncture has become becoming widely known and used. In addition there are some people called "energy workers" who can see a person's aura with their naked eye. These people have devised modalities to enhance the wellness of the bio-plasmic body with a consequent increase in a person's health and well-being. According to their information it is impossible to have a healthy physical body without having a healthy bio-plasmic body. As an example of the usefulness of their system, a simple tapping modality advocated by one of these energy workers at certain acupuncture points can purify the lymphatic system so that the possibility of breast cancer in women is virtually eliminated. Two of these American energy workers who have written extensively about this are Donna Eden and Barbara Brennan. Both are said to be able to see energy bodies around the human body with their naked eye.

An outline of the primary spiritual centers and matching endocrine glands follows.

Spiritual Center	Endocrine Gland	Sanskrit Name of Chakra	Meaning
7.	Pituitary	Ashasrara	Holy void of silence
6.	Pineal	Ana	Authority, command, power
5.	Thyroid	Vishuddha	Pure
4.	Thymus	Anahata	Unstricken

3.	Adrenal	Manipura	The city of gems
2.	Lyden	Svadhisthan	Dwelling place of the self
1.	Gonads	Muladhara	Foundation

The spiritual centers are not in the physical body, but what is called the ethereal body.

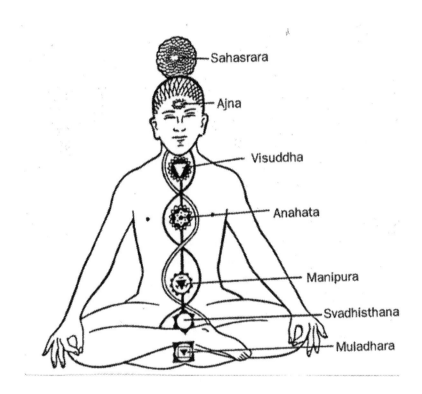

The seven spiritual centers interface with the seven glands in the endocrine system.

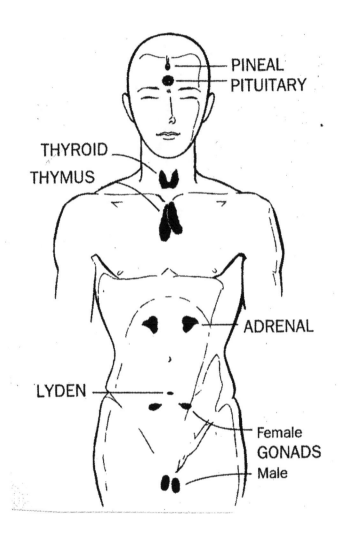

The bio-plasmic body may be seen graphically in the following way.

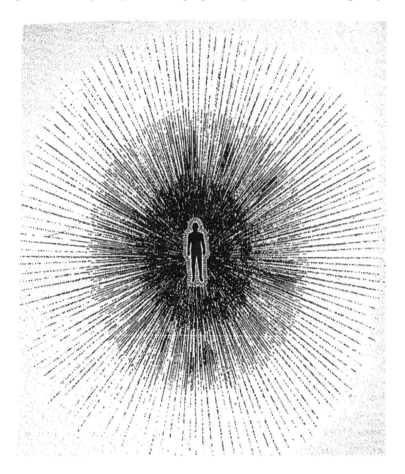

As may be deduced, the higher the chakra or gland in the body, the more refined it is. The center where physical life begins is in the gonads, but there is minimal intelligence there. That isn't to say that there is no intelligence at the lower levels, as scientists have found brain cells in all parts of the body. The seventh, or highest chakra, functions at the most refined level and is closest to the source of divinity. In Buddhist meditation, energy moves through the chakras with the object being attunement at the highest center, which is known as "entering into the silence". Energy moves between the chakras through what is known as kundalini. Edgar Cayce, has described a system of optimal energy movement that is somewhat different from this. It centers on the third, or adrenal center, with the energy moving between the chakras in a figure eight. This channel of energy is like a snake and it is meaningful that a snake, or the medusa, is the symbol for healing in the medical profession.

The ultimate purpose of these bodies with higher vibrations, the mental, emotional, and spiritual, is to engender universal virtue among all people. This is the quality of Christ consciousness that Edgar Cayce has described and the Bible a story of how this is to be achieved. The simplest example of seeing how spiritual energy may be raised in the seven-fold pattern in the Bible has been shown by Edgar Cayce to be the Lord's Prayer.

Spiritual

Center

7   Our Father who art in heaven

6   Hallowed be thy name

5   Thy kingdom come, they will be done

      on earth as it is in heaven

1   Give us this day our daily bread

3   And forgive us our debts as we forgive others

2   And lead us not into tribulation

4   But deliver us from evil

7,6,5 For thine is the kingdom and the power and the glory forever.

It becomes obvious that in all instances of the seven-fold structure, there are common characteristics to each level. Seven is the number of completeness or spiritual perfection in Biblical mathematics. As described in "Biblical Mathematics" by evangelist Ed F. Vallowe, the number seven has the following characteristics. "On the Day of Atonement, the priest sprinkled the mercy seat seven times. The Israelites marched around Jericho seven times. There were seven feast days of our Lord. There were seven branches on the candlestick in the tabernacle. Naaman washed seven times in the Jordan. The Savior spoke seven words from the cross. In the book of Daniel, Nebuchadnezzar had the furnace heated seven times hotter for the three Hebrew children." Physiologists say that the human body is recreated entirely via cell decay and reproduction every seven years. Like a diamond that has many facets, sevens occur in scripture and in nature with a myriad of juxtapositions. The following chart shows some manifestations of the seven-fold pattern that Edgar Cayce gave.

	Church in Revelation	Seal in Revelation	Ancient Element	Beasts in Revelation	Color	Musical Note
7	Laodicea	Silence			Violet	Ti
6	Philadelphia	Upheavals			Indigo	La
5	Sardis	Souls Slain			Blue	Sol
4	Thyatira	Pale Horse	Air	Eagle	Green	Fa

3	Pergamos	Red Horse	Fire	Lion	Yellow	Mi
2	Smyrna	Black Horse	Water	Man	Orange	Re
1	Ephesus	White Horse	Earth	Calf	Red	Do

The author first observed that the Bible might have other incidences of this seven-fold pattern by noticing the position of the books of Psalms and Proverbs. They relate to music and wisdom, which would put them in the province of the fourth spiritual center - the heart chakra   Then it became evident that the first chakra is the concern of the first book of the Bible, Genesis. Then there was the fact that Matthew, the first book of the New Testament, is the seed of all that follows which would relate it to the first or base chakra also. John, the fourth book of the New Testament, is primarily concerned with love. His name means, "Beloved of God", and so it must relate to the fourth or heart chakra. Other correlations have confirmed that there is a connection between the Bible and the chakras of the ethereal body in the following manner.

Spiritual Center	Old Testament	The Gospels	Epistles to the Churches
7	Prophets	Acts	Thessalonians
6	Prophets	Acts	Colossians
5	Ecclesiastes	-	
	Song of Solomon	Acts	Philippians
4	Job-Proverbs	John	Ephesians
3	Joshua – Esther	Luke	Galatians
2	Exodus – Deuteronomy		
1	Genesis	Matthew	Romans

An example of the seven-fold pattern in the New Testament is the case of the epistles of Paul which were sent to seven churches. It can also be seen that Romans, the first epistle and seed of the epistles of the New Testament, relates to first or base chakra. The proposition that the books of the prophets seem to relate to two spiritual centers, the two highest ones, might seem strange, but close examination reveals that the prophetic books are all in two parts. In this scheme of things the book of Acts in the New Testament can be seen as related to the three highest chakras. Although this commentary is primarily concerned with the Old Testament, the same pattern exists in the New Testament.

Chapter Two - Genesis; The Seed of the Old Testament

The first spiritual center is called the base chakra. In the human body, it is related to the reproductive glands; the gonads and the testes. This is how a person is physically created, how the physical body is generated, and so it is appropriate that Genesis is the name of the first book of the Old Testament All subsequent virtue springs from it. The theme of Genesis is established in its first few verses where the concept of creation in seven days is presented. This is the first occurrence of the sevenfold pattern in the Bible. .

The Seven Days of Creation

Related Spiritual Center	Created on that Day
7	Rest
6	Animals after their kind, man, and plants
5	Sea creatures; whales, fish. Birds
4	Lights to rule the day and night, seasons
3	Dry ground and seas; seeds, grass, and fruit
2	Firmaments between waters, the sky
1	Creation begins, formless spirit, then light

The beginning of anything is as a gross entity and here that is the first day of creation. The meaning of "day "here is not the same as a passage of twenty-four, hours, it should just be seen more as a dispensation. It is written that on the first day the world was created formless and void and, "…then there was light". Edgar Cayce has said that this light was not daylight, but the birth of consciousness.[6] The second day is concerned with waters above and below the firmament and it is no coincidence that the second spiritual center is also concerned with water, it being associated with the leyden gland in the body. The third day, which saw the beginning of growing things and the producing of fruit, is related to the third chakra. This is the spiritual center which interfaces with the body where food is converted into energy. Lights were created on the fourth day, which is similar to the function of the fourth spiritual center, associated with the thymus gland. This is the heart chakra and it's concern is the light of love and understanding.

Seeing some of these correlations between the human body and the Bible in the book of Genesis reinforces the idea that one should be conscious of their spiritual bodies when reading scripture. This promotes health and well-being as these similarities were designed by the Creator of both the book and the body. On the fifth day higher life forms which utilized the physical light from the fourth day, emerged. Man, who was created in the image of his Maker, needed both light and lower life forms to exist, and he made his debut on the sixth day. It is written that God rested on the seventh day, which is symbolic of grace, or freedom from personal effort. This is like the Buddhist concept of "Entering into the silence".

The Creator of the universe and Author of Genesis arranged this story of mankind's beginnings into a seven-fold pattern to provide ease of comprehension about the seed of the body, the base energy center. An outline of it follows.

The Seven-fold Seed in Genesis

Spiritual Center	Characters	Qualities Created
7	Sons of Israel	Refined abilities
6	Jacob or Israel	Higher intelligence - Jacob means artificer
5	Isaac	Fruit from inherited wholeness
4	Abraham	Wholeness through following one true God
3	Sons of Noah thru Terrah	A form of godliness, but confusion at Babel
2	Noah	Purification through water
1	Adam thru Lamech	Basic creation as gross energy

Any system starts in the first step with unrefined energy. The steps of the growth of the plant are contained within the seed. The steps of the growth of the principles in the Bible are contained in its seed, Genesis. In seed of the Bible the code of the first step is contained in the stories from the creation of the first man, Adam, through the time of Lamech, the father of Noah. Adam was created on the sixth day and he lived in a perfect place where there were trees of different kinds which supplied whatever was needed. However, the first soul was told to not eat of the tree of the knowledge of good and evil. Despite having a seemingly perfect existence in the garden there was a problem – Adam was lonesome. So God caused a deep sleep to come upon him, and He took part of him to create woman, who was called Eve. Edgar Cayce has said that the deep sleep was a form of meditation that made life more profound and therefore enjoyable for man. This story is symbolic and somewhat childlike, but it is useful as a valid portrayal of the creation of the basic energy source in mankind. The seven spiritual centers are rotating vortices of energy and where the rotation is clock-wise for men, it is counter clock-wise for women.[7] This pertains throughout the seven chakras and it provides strength through the duality .of having two sexes. The creation myth being symbolic, the first couple were likely spiritual entities initially. However, they sinned when Eve had them eat of the tree of the knowledge of good and evil, and were made naked or separated from the Godhead. They then were provided with animal skins to cover their nakedness. These animal skins are likely the physical bodies that are to be used to regain a state of purity.

The second step in Genesis, like the second chakra in mankind, provides purification of the energy which was created in the first step. In Genesis this is the story of Noah and how he and seven others from his family overcame a flood in a large boat, called an ark. This step is related to water in both Genesis and the body where functioning is through the leyden gland which is associated with the second charka. The eight people in the ark symbolize new beginnings, which is meaning of the number eight in Biblical Mathematics.[8]

It says in Genesis that before the flood the sons of man saw that the daughters of man were fair and they took them as wives. The implication of this is that there was no purifying force yet, only raw energy, and it is obvious that the Creator doesn't like his creatures to remain like that. He doesn't like animism which only gratifies base instincts related to the first chakra. A person knows instinctively that, while normal desire is a positive force, it must be purified into something greater. Noah found grace in the sight of the Lord as a person must find it through find a purifying aspect which modifies their raw desires. The story of Noah, his family, and the animals in the ark symbolizes man, his elemental animal nature and family relationships which are purified through grace.

After purification of basic energy in step two, further growth continues in the next step. The function of step three is to produce fruitful results after purification. The offspring of Noah, who were purified through water in step two, were proficient in many ways. There was Nimrod, who grew to be a warrior and was said to be a mighty hunter before the Lord. And there were adventurous maritime people who created clans and nations. The descendents of Noah grew to be a great people. However, with their prosperity they became proud. This can be seen in their construction of the Tower of Babel, where progress up from the mire led to pride. It is written that the Most High saw the self-glorification in construction of the Tower and He was unhappy about it. From this it can be seen that true virtue is to be apprehended only from above and always through grace. God showed this at the Tower by confusing man's languages so that he would realize that he wasn't close to being godlike yet. Man learned through this that, although he is able to construct complex structures through abstraction, he is still only a few steps above an animal here.

The fourth step in Genesis concerns the story of Abraham. According to Edgar Cayce, purification of the mental aspect of man begins here, whereas before the concern was the physical. The fourth chakra is related to the heart, and Abraham was the first person with a pure enough heart to see that the Source of all virtue is unitary. Abraham came from the advanced but polytheistic city of Ur of the Chaldees, and he was the first one to see that focused virtue is better than diffuse and random energy. There is undirected energy in the chakras before this step, but it becomes focused in the heart chakra. Edgar Cayce has said that starting with Abraham the concern of the Bible is the mental body of man whereas before only the physical body was addressed. This might seem confusing at first as the had is often thought of as the only mental center. It has been found, however, that there are brain cells in all portions of the physical body, so a person can have energy in these areas, such as the heart, that is truly mental.

The fifth chakra is associated with the thyroid gland, the location of which is in the throat and the fifth step in purification of spiritual energy in Genesis is associated with complex speech. After the purifying of human motives, which was accomplished through Abraham, his son Isaac utilized a refined form of energy to enjoy a full life. "Isaac" means laughter, which implies the enjoyment of a higher state of existence, something which involves more freedom. Isaac prospered in the setting that his progenitor secured for him by leaving the polytheistic city of Ur. He enjoyed his outdoor desert life in Canaan far away from the pagan nation from which his father came.

Jacob, next in the line of the patriarchs, represents purification of the sixth charka. His name means "deceiver" or "artificer, which indicates that he didn't deal with simple concepts. He used his extended ability to deceive his carnal brother, Esau, out of his birthright, something which represents a person gaining dominion over their lower nature through higher intelligence. He became a new and more refined person when he wrestled with an angel before confronting his carnal brother, and afterwards he was known as Israel.

The most refined entity in Genesis is the family of Israel, all of whom had some unique quality. These qualities were recounted by Jacob on his deathbed as recorded in chapter forty-nine of Genesis. Jacob had twelve sons and that number symbolizes governmental perfection in Biblical Mathematics, something which confirms that the seed in Genesis has now ascended to its highest step in these twelve individuals. There are twelve pairs of cranial nerves in the human head, and this is the place where the pituitary gland is located. This gland interfaces with the seventh charka, and mankind has its closest relationship with his Creator there. The following charts give further information about correlations between the Bible and the mental nature of mankind. The information about the attributes of the sons of Israel comes from "A Commentary on the Book of Revelation" by the A.R.E. Press, the publishing firm of the Edgar Cayce organization.[9]

Gad
Attraction
Cells

Reuben
Perpetuation
Circulation

Zebulon
Light
Digestion

Judah
Preservation
Assimilation

Joseph
Soul
Covering

Manasseh
Power
Elimination

Benjamin
Will
Bones

Naphtali
Opportunity
Nerve

Simeon
Desire
Organs

Asher
Life
Lymph

Levi
Decision
Glands

Issachar
Conscience
Membranes

Cranial Nerves

Tongue
Movements

Head
Movements

Olfactory

Vagas

Optic

Taste
Swallowing

Oculomotor

Vestibulo-
cochlear

Troclear

Facial

Trigemenial

Abducens

This summarizes the content of Genesis and how the book relates to the person who reads it. It has been shown that it is a reflection of its name, the generator of basic energy and its effect is on the lowest spiritual center, the first chakra. In reading and absorbing its lessons, one will have their base energy source enhanced. This book, like a seed in nature is complete in itself, and yet it has within it the pattern of that which is to follow. The genetic code in Genesis is in the form of a seven-fold structure and there is also an occurrence of a twelve-fold pattern.

Chapter Three - Energy from Genesis is Refined

After the basic energy source was established in Genesis, something which relates to the first chakra, it proceeds to more refined levels in the book and the body. These can be seen in the following books of the Old Testament.

Spiritual Center	Books of the Bible
5	Ecclesiastes, Song of Solomon
4	Job, Psalms, Proverbs
3	Joshua, Judges, Ruth, I & II Samuel, I & II Kings, I & II Chronicles, Ezra, Nehemiah Esther
2	Exodus, Leviticus, Numbers, Deuteronomy

In the human body after energy is generated in the first chakra, which has a parallel in Genesis, energy proceeds to a place of purification through water. This is the function of the leyden gland. The books from Exodus through Deuteronomy relate to this function which is connected with the second spiritual center. The concern of Exodus is the departure of the Hebrews through the Red Sea from the fecund and yet carnal land of Egypt. This is like the activity in the second chakra, the purpose of which is to cleanse the raw the raw energy from the first spiritual center with water.

The books relating to the second spiritual center then should be looked upon not as historical records, but as a source of purification through more refined consciousness. By following the activity of the Hebrews in their exodus from Egypt it is possible to visualize the proper flow of energy through the second spiritual center. The Hebrews' departure from Egypt first involved Moses sounding a multi-faceted warning to the leader of Egypt, Pharaoh. Then there was a selection of the chosen people through the blood of a lamb, and finally a journey through the Red Sea which eliminated the antagonistic Egyptians. Egypt should be seen as a symbol of carnal energy and exodus from it as progress above base human motives according to Edgar Cayce.[10] Going through the Red Sea to escape the Egyptians in this step is a validation of its being related to the second chakra, which is also concerned with water.

Purification, besides leaving carnal Egypt in the exodus, also involves codification of principles relating to this. This may be seen in the laws spelled out in the books of Leviticus, Numbers, and Deuteronomy. Having these laws provides a stable footing from which to proceed into more refined energy states.

After purification of energy in step two of the Old Testament and in the body, the energy flow continues into a place of conflict. For a person this is a place of dynamism related to the adrenal area, the source of energy for the body. Attunement of this spiritual center involves utilizing the digestive system in an efficient manner. It entails having faith that this source of natural energy functions according to the design of its Source, and is being maintained in a gracious manner. In the books of the Old Testament relating to this third spiritual center the primary theme is ruling in the fecund land of Canaan. This can be seen in the arrival of the chosen people there under the leadership of Joshua. The books from Joshua through Esther are primarily a record of the ebb and flow of politics and war in the promised land. First Joshua took possession of the land of plenty through warfare with the native Canaanites. Then there were battles led by Israel's judges against the remaining carnal forces. After that, the kings of Israel and Judah ruled through continuing conflict as recorded in I & II Samuel, I & II Kings, and I & II Chronicles. The fact that there are three records of the same time period likely represents the triune nature of God and man. Then the books of Ezra and Jeremiah recount the history of Israel during restoration from captivity in Babylon. The final book relating to this spiritual center of energy is Esther, where the message of the one true God of Israel is conveyed to the rest of the known world. This is a portent of spiritual energy being refined into a higher state in the next step.

The books of the Old Testament relating to the fourth spiritual center likely start with Job. According to Edgar Cayce that book illustrates one's life journey. It is a story about faith and patience overcoming a seemingly impossible human situation. Job initially had a beneficial situation, with everything going his way, until Satan was loosed on him. Then he had to endure tests in all areas of his life, until he finally emerged victorious. At the end he had an even more favorable situation than he started with. Job was a good man, but there was an element of pride about him that had to be eliminated. This was done through suffering, until he saw that his virtue compared with that of his Creator, was infinitesimal. In seeing this one can relate to the flow of events in their life, starting when they are young and innocent. They must realize that they must grow though hardships while eliminating their pride.

The following books of Psalms and Proverbs definitely relate to the fourth spiritual center and their primary concerns are beauty and wisdom. That these books follow Job is logical because there must be suffering and testing before there can be an appreciation of beauty and wisdom. The Psalms are poetry set to music, and Proverbs is concerned with wisdom, the proper way in which one should conduct their affairs. Both books are of an artistic nature, designed to develop the fourth spiritual center, but only as they are used as a channel and not to enhance the ego.

Psalm 23 is an example of raising energy in the seven–step pattern.

Spiritual

Center

7,6,5   The Lord is my shepherd, I shall not want.

1   He makes me to lie down in green pastures,

2   He leads me beside still waters,

3   He restores my soul.

4   Yea, through I walk through the valley of the shadow of death I will fear

      no evil, for you art with me. Your rod and staff comfort me.

5   You prepare a table before me in the presence of my enemies.

6   You anoint my head with oil, my cup runs over.

7   Surely goodness and mercy shall follow me all the days of my life, and I

      shall dwell in the house of the Lord forever.

There is a prayer of indigenous people of America in the same pattern.

Spiritual

Center

7,6,5   O Great Spirit whose voice I hear in the wind and whose breath gives

      life to all the world.

1   Hear me because I am small and weak and need your strength and

      wisdom.

2   Let me walk in beauty and let my eyes ever behold the red and purple

      sunset

3   Make my hands respect the things You made and make my ears sharp

      to hear your voice.

4   Let me learn the lessons You have hidden in every rock and leaf

5   Make me wise that I may understand the things You've taught my

people.

6   Make me strong not that I may be greater than my brother, but so that I can fight my worst enemy, myself

7   Let me come to You with clean hands and a pure heart so that when life fades like the sunset I may come to You unashamed.

Psalm 24 uses this pattern also.

Spiritual

Center

1   The earth is the Lord's and its fullness, the world and all that's in it.

2   For He founded it on the waters, and established it on the seas.

3   Who shall ascend to mountain of the Lord , or who will dwell in His holy temple?

4   He who has clean hands and a pure heart, who does not lift up his soul to vanity nor swear deceitfully. He will receive blessings from the Lord and righteousness from the God of salvation.

5   This is the generation who seeks Him, who seeks the face of Jacob.

6   Lift up your heads, O ye gates; and be lifted up ye everlasting doors and the King of glory shall come in. Who is the King of Glory? The Lord strong and mighty, the Lord mighty in battle.

7   Lift up your heads, O ye gates; even lift them up ye everlasting doors, and the King of Glory shall come in. Who is this King of Glory? The Lord of Hosts, he is the King of Glory.

The second step in both Psalms 23 and 24 refers to water, which is a validation of the chakra pattern in them. In this regard the gates and doors in Psalm 24 likely refer to the chakras themselves and the connection between them, kundalini energy. There are other verses in the Psalms which also lead one to believe that they are concerned with the spiritual centers of mankind. Psalm 19 says, "The precepts of the Lord are right, giving joy to the heart. The commands of the Lord are radiant, enlightening the eyes."   This is a likely reference to the heart chakra, and how it is energized through seeing the beauty of the written word. And, Psalm 91 begins, "He that dwelleth in the secret place of the Most High shall abide under the shadow of the Almighty." This is likely a reference to the unlimited spiritual virtue in the highest chakra, the seventh.

There are other patterns that are significant in the Psalms and Proverbs which relate to the sequence of their chapters. Psalm one is an admonition to purification of one's motives, and in the last Psalm, one-hundred-fifty, energy has ascended to its highest level where only praise is appropriate   The Proverbs start with a tribute to the value of wisdom and they end with a symbol of perfect wisdom, a virtuous woman, the ultimate nurturer. As any observer may attest, the natural human heart is impure, and devious and a convenient way to achieve purification of the fourth spiritual center is to read Psalms and Proverbs. Some dedicated people have advocated reading at least one psalm and one chapter of the Proverbs every day. This would be good for attuning the fourth charka.

The fifth spiritual center, or throat chakra, is concerned with the will and spoken word, something consonant with this center being developed through the next book, Ecclesiastes, a name which means, "The Preacher".   While Psalms and Proverbs are artistic and raise spiritual energy in the fourth chakra, Ecclesiastes is an exhortation to use this energy to lead a life which is worthwhile. Tit is a sermon about having the wisdom to lead a constructive life, yet it ends on a mixed note of despair and hope. The despair comes from the fact that even though a person may lead a good life and diligently take care of their affairs they will ultimately still die. This is expressed in an exhortation to value life highly before, "...the silver cord is severed, or the golden bowl is broken."   This is likely a reference to the end of the physical body which is dependent on the silver cord, which is likely the channel of kundalini energy. And the golden bowl referred to is likely the cranium, which contains the center of the highest chakras.

While there is despair in the book of the Ecclesiastes through seeing one's inevitable demise, there is hope in knowing that there are greater worlds than can be physically or mentally conceived of. This hope comes through seeing that energy can be raised to higher levels and one doesn't have to remain in a physical or mental prison forever. It may also be seen that while a person lives they can ascend to higher and more refined energy levels through attunement of their higher chakras. The book following Proverbs, The Song of Solomon, also gives hope for ascendance to a higher level. In it a female narrator is searching for her lover to bring her satisfaction. This is symbolic of the sensitive female aspect of personality looking for assistance in being raised to a higher state. It doesn't appear obvious what this higher state will be because the books of the Ecclesiastes and the Song of Solomon seem to be the epitome of the use of words that may be used to raise spiritual energy in the ethereal body. However, looking forward to the books of the prophets in the Old Testament this hope is fulfilled in a unique and profound way.

Chapter Four - The Prophets, More Refined Functioning

The remaining books of the Old Testament were written by the prophets. There are sixteen of them, all written from 840 B.C.E. to 432 B.C E.. A perceptive person will not see them as history, however.   Like the preceding books of the Old Testament, their main purpose is the attunement of man's spiritual centers, his ethereal body. If the Creator of time and space had wanted a series of books to be written about a series of events they would of course had a proper time sequence, and yet the books of the prophets are not of this form. Some of the prophetic books which come earlier in the sequence of the canon happened later in history, and so there must be an organizational format other than the historical. A pattern does appear which is not time-dependent. There are four books which have been called the major prophets and they can be seen to address aspects of human nature. This can be seen to advance the idea that the major prophets address more basic functioning as four is the number of the world in Biblical mathematics. Then there are twelve books which have been called minor prophets and they can be seen to address certain psychological aspects. This fact would promote the impression that they are concerned with more refined concepts than the major prophets as twelve is the number of governmental perfection in Biblical mathematics. These twelve books then must be concerned with pure mental processes.

The proposition that the prophetic books are other than the recounting of history is supported by the system of seven spiritual centers that has already been seen. The system of chakras in mankind, and the Old Testament, appear as parallels and thus the prophetic books then must address the two highest chakras, the sixth and seventh. This theory can be verified through seeing that the books of the prophets all appear to be in two parts thus addressing the two highest spiritual centers. In seeing this, one should be aware that the books of the prophets take up where the prior books of Ecclesiastes, and the Song of Solomon left off. Those books addressed the fifth chakra and were the epitome in the use of language and great wisdom. The books of the prophets, however, contain something greater. They use symbols or archetypes rather than words with literal meanings and so have an impact at a higher level. The books of the prophets in the Old Testament then go beyond the recounting of history or the use of beautiful language or poetry, they are symbolic. the prophetic books then address the sixth and seventh chakras in a new way.   The idea that the prophetic books are other than the recounting of historical events is not new, having been advanced by such Bible scholars as J. Vernon McGee.[11]   The symbolic nature of the prophetic books is readily seen when viewing them as addressing the sixth and seventh chakras. In this system a person tries to follow fixed behavior patterns at the level of the sixth spiritual center while at the level of the seventh there is only receptiveness and grace.

The nature of the prophetic books may be seen in that all relate to characteristics of nations, or geo-political entities such as Judah, Israel, Jerusalem, Babylon, and Assyria. These names should be seen as personal proclivities in the universal psyche, instead of physical places. As the quote by Edgar Cayce has pointed out, places are also conditions, circumstances, and experiences to a person. In this context, for example, the people of Israel should be seen as having the those who consider themselves chosen, and Jerusalem should be seen as the most holy center of such people. In this context, any people can decide to be one of the chosen, to make the journey of enlightenment in their higher nature. The prophetic books, as has been stated, have meanings which are greater than the simple word forms which were used in the prior books in the cannon. Here, complex images are used which are usually geo-physical place names. Throughout the prophetic books, places in the holy land, such as Jerusalem, Judah, Israel, symbolize aspects of the human psyche which are ordained to be pure. And in the same manner, it may be seen that Babylon represents the ego, Assyria represents the carnal "monkey mind", and Egypt represents the flesh state.

These symbolic names are resident at the levels of the sixth and seventh chakras. The dynamic in the books of the prophets then is; condemnation of some personal proclivities at the level of the sixth chakra, and resolution of this at the level of the seventh chakra. After resolution there is only quiet and receptivity at the level of the highest spiritual center. When a person is functioning at higher mental levels, there is the probability that they will succumb to egotism and so be guilty of attitudes and behaviors which are not present when functioning as less profound levels. The condemnations in the first part of all the prophetic books then are generally for corrections of errors of egotism which must be addressed before the silence and receptivity at the seventh spiritual center is achieved.

The dual nature of the prophetic books is especially pronounced in some of them. Virtually all scholars agree that there are two portions of Isaiah. Chapters one through thirty-nine were obviously written at a different time than chapters forty through sixty-six. The book of Daniel also clearly has two parts. In the first part, Daniel a man, prophesied to another man, the king. In the second part, an angel prophesied to a man, Daniel. Joel is also in two parts, the first being a time of tribulation for the nation of Israel, and the second part a time of comfort. Jonah also has two distinct parts; the first before he was swallowed by a whale and the second after he repented and was deposited on land. While not always as evident in the others, the prophetic books can be seen to be in two parts.

The prophetic books, while appearing to have a dual nature, can also be looked upon as having a triune dynamic. The first step is condemnation of some aspect or aspects of a geo-political entity, the second step a time of change, and the third a state of hope and affirmation. This would relate to a person as condemnation of personal proclivities at the level of the sixth chakra, raising of spiritual energy to a higher level through repentance, and finally acceptance and attunement to the Lord's will at the level of the seventh chakra. While having this dynamic, the prophetic books each address a different psychological aspect. The major prophets; Isaiah, Jeremiah, Ezekiel, and Daniel, are concerned with four specific facets of human functioning. The individual aspects of these books are that Isaiah relates to mental functioning, Jeremiah, the emotional, Ezekiel to the physical, and Daniel to governing. Then there are twelve books of the minor prophets which can be seen as portraying a system of continuous psychological states

Isaiah is definitely concerned with the mental function in the human psyche. "The New Bible Commentary" says, "God reasons with man – that is the first article of religion according to Isaiah."[12] That commentary also reports how frequently the words "know" "consider", and" reason" are used in Isaiah. Jeremiah is known as the "Weeping Prophet", mainly for his emotional concern over the condition of the holy city of Jerusalem. It is written in Jeremiah, "The human heart is deceitful above all things and desperately wicked. Who can known it?" The purpose of Jeremiah then is to achieve a pure emotional dynamic so as to use the mental energy achieved in Isaiah.

A third aspect of mankind, the physical, is the concern of Ezekiel. His prophecy starts with an image of four creatures and four wheels while he was in Babylon. The physical world is represented in Biblical mathematics by the number four, so this is an indication of the nature of his prophecy. Ezekiel, dealing with physical strengthening in the world, would then logically follow Isaiah and Jeremiah which deal with mental and emotional aspects. While learning in the abstract is of some value, putting mental and emotional energy into effect Is necessary and this is what is to be done in Ezekiel. The prophet Ezekiel also deals with the physical nature of the holy temple which was to be built in Jerusalem. Then comes the book of Daniel, the prophet who has been called apocalyptic. The word apocalyptic means revelation, the calling forth of something that was hidden. Daniel may be looked upon as calling forth the qualities that were attained in the preceding three prophecies, something done through the ruling faculty of mankind. The hallmark of the book of Daniel is the concern for personal, and worldwide dominion.

After the four books of the major prophets there are twelve books which are called minor prophets. This is appropriate, as they are the last books of the Old Testament and twelve is the number of divine completion in Biblical mathematics. Twelve also symbolizes governmental perfection and the nation of Israel.[13] This number was previously seen in the sons of Jacob at the end of Genesis, the seed of the Bible, and it is significant that there are twelve paired nerves in the human cranium. As has been noted, Edgar Cayce said that the Bible, starting with Abraham addresses the mental functioning of man and in the minor prophets that dynamic has reached its most refined level.

The books of the prophets are diagrams of the ideal way for a person to function through their higher faculties. The major prophets address man's mental, emotional, physical, and governing functions and the minor prophets then address his psychological functioning. It has been proposed by psychologists that man functions through a circular pattern with a constantly changing mental focus. This is in line with psychological thought which sees archetypes as the key to this process. This may be seen in the work of psychologist Dr. Carol S. Pearson who used the number six in a continuous system of psychological focus in her first book, "The Hero Within.[14] In a later book, "Awakening the Hero within", she used the number of twelve for basically the same process. The twelve books of the minor prophets can be seen to use a similar system of psychological states. While Dr. Pearson has expounded this system to enhance the quality of a person's functioning, utilizing the same system from the inspired writings of scripture promises added benefits because of the sacred nature of these books.

The book where Dr. Pearson has delineated a system of six archetypes for psychological functioning is "The Hero Within".

The following is a diagram of Dr. Pearson's system in "The Hero Within".

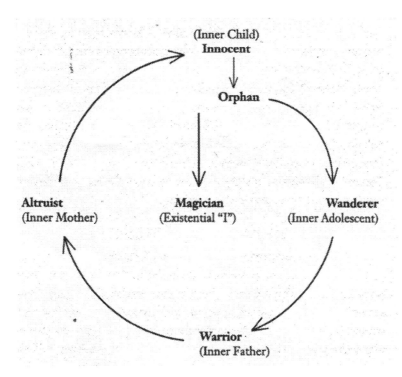

The system of continuous archetypes Dr. Pearson used in "The Hero Within", is similar to the system which may be seen in the minor prophets.

Minor Prophets Personal Attributes

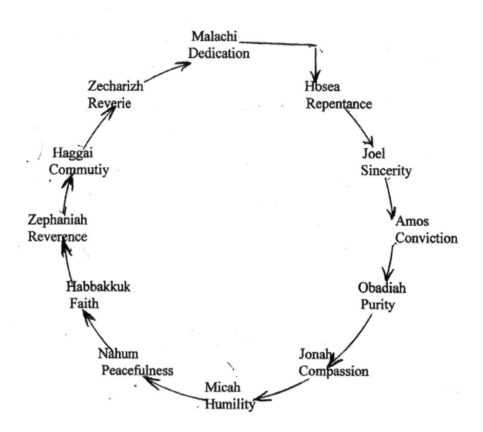

A qualification for addressing the higher realms of the psyche is that they be regarded with awe and respect. When done correctly, studying the prophetic books in light of their symbolic meanings may produce considerable personal benefits. There is always a battle for attunement at the level of the sixth chakra and then grace for a person when there is acceptance at the level of the seventh chakra. If, as proposed, the prophetic books define the basic way in which a person functions through various aspects, they should be studied in detail and valued for their benefits. This proposition is supported by the many references to them in the New Testament. Acceptance through grace in the prophetic books looks towards the coming of the messiah in the New Testament. It is well to remember, in this regard that the messiah is the cornerstone, while the foundation of the house of God has been declared in scripture to be those specifically called by God, especially the prophets.[15]

Chapter Five - The Major Prophets

Historical Information about the Major Prophets

Prophet	Personal Aspect	Place of Prophecy	Concern of the of the Prophet
Isaiah	*Mind*	Jerusalem	Assyria until the end of Israel, then Babylon
Jeremiah	*Emotions*	Judah and Egypt	The people of Judah must go to Babylon
Ezekiel	*Physical*	Babylon	Decadence of the holy places
Daniel	*Governing*	Babylon	Principles of governing

Psychological Meanings of the Major Prophets

Isaiah	Resist the carnal mind and then deal with the ego
Jeremiah	Realize one has carnal emotions and driven by the ego
Ezekiel	A pure mind strengthens the body
Daniel	Ordained rules must be followed

There are four books called the major prophets and four in Biblical Mathematics is the number of the world. This supports the premise that they are each concerned with a different human function: Isaiah with the reasoning aspect, Jeremiah the emotional, Ezekiel the physical, and Daniel ruling.

Isaiah (Yahweh Saves) The Mind

The book of Isaiah is concerned with the refinement of the mental processes everyone uses. Its starting point is the level of the fifth chakra where the previous book of Ecclesiastes, the preacher, left off. Truth was addressed there, but not at a very profound level. This is seen in Isaiah 1:3 which is, "The ox knoweth his owner, and the ass his master; but Israel doth not know, my people doth not consider." Up to this point in the Old Testament one has only been exposed to animistic reasoning, parroting praise, and selfish wisdom. The ox and ass are obedient to directions from their master, but until this level a person has not truly related to his Master. To function at this more profound level one must use complex images or archetypes instead of words. The Jungian analyst, John Sanford, has said that forms such as these bypass the bottleneck of the ego.[16] The motive for addressing concepts at these higher levels is described next; it is imperative. This irrevocable calling to a more profound state of mental functioning is described in Isaiah 2:1 through 4:6 and it is known as, "The day of the Lord". The meaning of this for a person was described by Edgar Cayce when he was asked about a person's relation to such concepts as dreams or complex images. He said, "The negligence of its associations, both physical, mental, and spiritual, indicates a very negligible personage."[17] There is the point in the development of the mind where simple methods of functioning are condemned, and in Isaiah this is called, "The day of the Lord".

Next in Isaiah it is said that all nations would be rebuked, which means that all personal mental aspects would be tried. This may be seen in the quote from Edgar Cayce, which indicates that geo-political entities, such as nations, have personal meanings also. It is said here that all nations would go to Judah, Jerusalem, and Mount Zion, which is the "Mountain of the Lord". A mountain in scripture is generally considered to be a people group so the meaning here is that all personal mental attributes will be tested for purity in relationships. Judah, Jerusalem, and Mount Zion should be considered sacred places, reflecting areas in the human psyche which are ordained to be pure. Then it is said that nation shall not lift up sword against nation any more, which means that at this new level of meaning, personal conflicts cannot be resolved violently. The timing of this day of the Lord is not known but the Source of the plan of purification has given assurances that He is patient and compassionate. From this it can be seen that what was lost in meaning at the Tower of Babel will eventually be restored, and confusion and accusations implicit in human languages are eliminated when at this more profound level. Personal mental purification and nation cleansing are related, and both will be found imperative at some time. That is why it is necessary for a person to function at the levels of the sixth and seventh chakra where complex and universal images, such as archetypes, are the currency.

The first half of Isaiah, before chapter forty, contains prophecies concerning certain geopolitical entities. Through following them it is possible to determine the characteristics of the people groups mentioned and get a map of the mental process which are used when functioning at the level of the sixth chakra. As has been said, the first part of all the prophecies relates to the sixth chakra, and the second part to functioning at the level of the highest spiritual center. A source for seeing the relation of political names to personal tendencies is "Thru the Bible", by J. Vernon McGee.[18] Purification of mental functioning is seen here in prophecies against Assyria, which symbolizes the carnal "monkey mind", and Egypt, which personifies the flesh state. The proposition that Assyria represents the carnal mind which has excessive nationalistic fervor, comes from the history of that nation in antiquity. At one time Assyria conquered all the nations around it except Judah. They did this by using excessive fervor and showing no mercy to any of their foes. They would do such things as skin their enemies alive, and bury them in sand up to their necks so they would roast to death. They were certainly nationally dedicated, while at the same time certainly excessive in fervor. Babylon was a rich and powerful nation that has been said to symbolize the ego, and prophecies about it in Isaiah are for refinement of that attribute in mental functioning. A validation of the thesis about nations in general and Babylon in particular is that Edgar Cayce is recorded as saying, "Babylon symbolizes self."[19]

Prophecies about other personal mental attributes can be seen starting in chapter eleven of Isaiah. There it is said that there will be a rod out of the stem of Jesse and quiet understanding. This symbolizes the hope of enlightened ruling as Jesse was the father of David, the great king of Israel. It is also said that the wolf and the lamb would lie down together, symbolizing a mental state which is neither overly aggressive nor outstandingly placid. Then it is said that the leopard and kid would dwell together, symbolizing a condition where neither stealth nor simple-mindedness is the overriding mentality. Chapter fourteen describes the situation where mercy is afforded to Jacob and Lucifer is fallen. Jacob, whose name means "deceiver", symbolizes mental adroitness and Lucifer is a symbol of perversity and so this is a condition where effective thinking overcomes tendencies towards perverse impulses. These are a few of the principles of sound thinking in the first part of Isaiah's prophecy.

A specific example of mental purification in chapter thirty-one starts with a proclamation of woe on those who would go down to Egypt and rely on horses and chariots. Since Egypt is a symbol of the flesh state, and horses symbolize carriers of specific qualities, this is an injunction against resorting to carnal forces when attempting to function at more profound mental levels. Chapter thirty-two, the next step in purification of mental functioning, describes the reward for this. It is said that a king would reign in righteousness and princes would rule with justice. This represents a mental pattern where integrity allows one to govern their affairs intelligently. The reward for making this a habit is then spelled out. It is said that, "The Spirit is poured upon us from on high, and the wilderness becomes a fruitful field, and the fruitful field is valued as a forest."

Chapter thirty-five is where the promise of functioning through the higher mind, at the level of the seventh charka, is given. Here the end of attempts at carnal human reasoning is prophesized. It is said that then the desert would be a paradise, the lame would run like a deer, and the dumb would sing. This is certainly not a physical description, but it represents ascendance to the mental level where there is only receptivity from a higher Source, and all personal defects have been eliminated.

Chapters thirty-six through thirty-nine are concerned historically with the Jewish resistance to an invasion by the Assyrian King Sennacherib. This symbolizes using one's higher nature to resist excessive undirected mental functioning. Historically Assyria was ruthless and had defeated all the surrounding nations except Judah. The Assyrians represent the proclivity for a person to use their slightly mad "monkey mind" instead of divine reason. King Sennacherib of Assyria demanded surrender from God's chosen people, and as he had defeated all other nations, it seemed futile to resist him. However, King Hezekiah of Judah, with the help of the prophet, Isaiah, found out through prayer that the Assyrians were ordained to be destroyed and on this basis he resisted them. This represents the denial of egoistic mental energy at the level of the sixth chakra, and achievement of functioning in the quiet of the seventh chakra.

After victory over the mad "monkey mind", starting in chapter forty of Isaiah, comfort and deliverance are decreed for the chosen people. For a person this represents mental functioning at the level of the seventh chakra. It is represented by those residing in Judah and Jerusalem. Also, it is said that they would ascend the holy mountain of Zion and would be of the Lord. This refers to those willing to ascend to the silence of the seventh chakra. For a person reading Isaiah this is where excessive undirected mental energy has been subdued and divine quiet and divine mental energy have taken over. At this point there is a lack of striving, something which has been called in Buddhism, "Entering into the silence". One is then stilled by awe and holy fear. This is seen in Isaiah 40:3, which is, "Prepare the way of the Most high...". Isaiah 40:6 is, "All flesh is as grass. The grass withereth, the flower fadeth, but the word of the Lord remaineth forever." Isaiah 40:13 asks, "Who has measured the waters? Who has directed the spirit?" In chapter forty and beyond deliverance from one's carnal mental nature gives pure mental functioning.

Significant in Isaiah are the passages which concern the Messiah. These are places where calm and enhanced mental energy is available through the reception of undeserved favor. The nature of these statements can be seen in Isaiah 7:14 which tells of a virgin being with child who will be called Immanuel, or "God with us". This is an image of virtue coming out of apparent nothingness, illustrating the principle of undeserved favor. The virgin, symbolizing pure motives, brings forth virtue without an apparent source. Virtually all promises of messianic intercession come in the second part of Isaiah's prophecy, so it can be seen that grace comes primarily through receptivity at the level of the highest chakra.

Prophecies about the Messiah in Isaiah [20]

Prophecy that The Messiah;	Reference	What is Represented
Will be born of a virgin	7:14	Grace comes without personal effort
Will be a light to all, and a Galilean	9:1,2	Grace is for all and from a common source
Will be an heir to the throne of David	9:7	Grace is ordained to have authority in a person
Will have his way prepared	40:3-5	There must be repentance before intercession
Will be spat upon and struck	50:6	The initial reaction to grace is negative
Will be exalted	53:13	Messianic grace is ordained to be victorious

Will be disfigured by suffering	52:14, 53:2	The messiah pays the price for all
Will make a blood atonement	53,5	His sacrifice will be for all
Will be widely rejected	53, 1,3	Grace is usually looked down upon
Will bear our sorrows and sins	53:4,5	Grace is useful for all mental states
Will be our substitute	53:6,8	Grace takes away negativity without effort
Will be buried in a rich man's tomb	53:9	Messianic grace is of infinite value
Will save all who believe in him	53:10,11	Messianic grace gives full assurance
Will die with transgressors	53:12	Messianic grace appears erroneous to the world system
Will heal the brokenhearted	61:1,2	Messianic grace gives a new perspective

When these passages are compared to the record of the historical Jesus, there is a realization the fulfillment of these prophecies in his ministry which gives peace of mind and increased mental effectiveness

Jeremiah (Exaltation of Yahweh) Emotions

Isaiah ends on the high note of all coming to worship the Lord, and then comes the book of Jeremiah and a seeming end to all of this positive energy. This is because, as has been seen, Isaiah is concerned with mental energy and Jeremiah is about the emotional aspect of mankind. Both prophetic books affect the two highest chakras.

Jeremiah's historical message was that the decadent nation of Judah should surrender to Babylon and the Jews temporarily leave their pure and beloved homeland for captivity in Babylon. Babylon has been seen as a symbol of the ego and Jeremiah wrote from both Judah and exile in Egypt, which country is symbolic of the flesh state. The meaning of this for a person then is that they should be aware that they are in a carnal abode and although they may know of a purer state, they must function through the ego, or self-analysis. This can be verified in that the exile of the chosen people in Babylon was to be for seventy years, the Biblical human life span. A person's proper attitude then should be one of contrition for behavior which has resulted in residence in a carnal, unsteady dwelling while having knowledge of a purer state. With such a mindset, one is able to effectively monitor one's emotions, which is the overall purpose of Jeremiah. " Any prophet like Jeremiah, whose concern is the emotional nature of mankind would certainly be a weeping one because of the foolishness of natural human emotions.

The sins of Judah and Israel are spelled out in the first half of Jeremiah's prophecy, something which is a condemnation of motivations which come from functioning at the level of the sixth chakra. Israel and Judah, the northern and southern kingdoms of the time, may be seen as symbolic of the sixth and seventh chakras respectively. A study of Jeremiah and his book of Lamentations is an emotionally purifying journey. A reasonable starting point for an analysis of Jeremiah is a statement in chapter two that the Lord has called his people out of Egypt, a nation which is symbolic of the flesh state. This was of course, under Moses and the Ten Commandments. The implication of this is that the people of Judah and Israel were historically the chosen people, and anyone can personally chose to be one of these. Then, in chapter three, there is an emphasis on the backsliding of God's chosen people. This can be seen as the revelation of deviant tendencies when trying to function at higher levels of meaning. While a person might be pure at lower levels, such as the using of beautiful words in the Psalms, yet when attempting to abstract at the level of the sixth chakra corrupt tendencies are revealed. Then it is easy to backslide and not assume one is as pure as they once did. To be pure at this level, one must be aware of the principle expressed in the Edgar Cayce statement that all increases in knowledge require a commensurate increase in humility. This is seen in chapter four of Jeremiah where the Lord demands that his people be clothed in sackcloth, and lament and howl before his fierce anger.

The emotional lamentation and mourning which is necessary to make progress at higher levels brings the restructuring of one's basic nature. It has been said that, while some healing may be accomplished by changes at lower levels, healing of the entire person comes through the highest chakras. This can be seen after chapter four in Isaiah where a change in one's attributes at higher levels brings about cleansing of the lower chakras, such as at the heart, adrenals, and gonads. Then it can be seen that purity of physical functioning comes from a pure mind using pure emotions. This brings the result which is spelled out in chapter seven – residence at the Lord's gate. For a person this implies coming near to a pure place in their emotions. This place is defined in the following chapters as one where there is no idolatry or vanity.

The cleansing of the chosen people in this prophecy is first accomplished through the prophet Jeremiah, and King, Josiah who reigned in Judah at that time. Jeremiah supported Josiah, the king who wanted to resurrect temple worship which was begun under Solomon. While doing so he found a Book of the Law, which had not been adhered to for a long time. This led to a revival in the people of Judah, the southern kingdom. However, in chapter twelve of Jeremiah's prophecy, the assassination of Josiah is described, and an evil period in the nation of Judah occurred where all hope for purification through the law or a good king was given up. This portends a descent into evil behavior. In chapters fourteen and fifteen the decadence of the nation of the chosen people has brought drought and famine. When all hope appeared to be gone, Jeremiah was told to declare a parable from the Lord - of a vessel made by a potter. This parable describes the only chance for hope among the chosen people - through grace, or undeserved favor.

The lowest point of Jeremiah's time as an emotional icon is described in chapter twenty where he, like some others in the Bible, curses the day he was born. This is where he sees no virtue in the nation of Judah, the chosen ones. Now, even the current king, Zedekiah, and all the supposedly noble people are corrupt and only functioning in selfishness. Then the only hope for the chosen people is surrender to Babylon, the symbol of the ego, or self-awareness. The emotional state of Jeremiah at this time can be looked upon in personal terms as "The dark night of the soul", where all hope seems gone. In this situation the only possibility for survival is grace or undeserved favor which engenders self-examination and correction of one's emotional nature.

The second part of the book of Jeremiah starts in chapter twenty-three. This part concerns activity in the seventh chakra. This higher level of functioning can be seen in such verses as Jeremiah 23:5 which mentions the Lord raising up a righteous Branch unto David. This will be a new king who shall reign and prosper, and execute judgment and justice in the earth. It is said that in the day of this king, Judah will be saved and Israel will dwell in safety. For a person this means that they, in their purest tendencies, should live in hope of the future ruler, who will be true and just. This enables a person to function in emotional viability no matter what the situation may be. From this point on in Jeremiah, peace, quiet, acceptance, and prosperity are destined, symbolic of a person functioning through grace in the seventh chakra. This is because one has stopped emotionally fighting one's destiny and instead functions through the will of the Lord of heaven and earth.

For the nation of Judah their destiny is described in chapter twenty-five as seventy years of captivity in Babylon. For a person this represents the achievement of humility so that they are able to function through self-analysis and continuing hope. This is because Babylon has been seen to represent the ego, and seventy years are representative of the normal human life span. Historically this was a time when king Nebuchadnezzar of Babylon, who was chosen by God, ruled the known world, something spelled out clearly in Jeremiah. It is also said that those Jews who might fight against captivity in Babylon would drink the wrath of God's fury.

Those who would accede to the prophesied seventy years of captivity were told that they could prosper; take wives, build houses, and plant gardens. This is to be a temporary situation though. It is said that the captives in Babylon, who represent people who achieve emotional stillness through self-examination, will finally return to their pure and beloved land of Judah. For a person this represents hope of the millennial age where the promised messiah will rule. While this hope is present in Jeremiah's prophecy, the prophet himself must spend some time in prison as his prophecies about captivity and eventual freedom do not meet with approval, especially among the power elite. Some of the Jews, seeing the difficulty of staying in Judah, or being captive in Babylon, choose to go to Egypt, a nation which represents the flesh state. These people do not prosper as they are going against the will of God which is that they should not regress to a lower state. Jeremiah himself prophesies about this to those who intend to go to Egypt.

The prophecy of Jeremiah contains declarations of judgments against many nations which surround the holy land of Judah, such as Egypt, Philistia, Moab, and Ammon. There are also condemnations of destruction on geo-political entities such as Edom, Bozrah, Kedar,

Hazar, and Damascus. It would require extensive scholarship to discern the nature of these ancient civilizations and their relation to the prophecy of Jeremiah as they relate to human emotions. The eventual overthrow of Babylon by the Medes and Persians is also prophesied. It is said that Babylon would pay a high price for the wrong that might be done to the nation of the chosen people while in a captive state. For a person this represents recompense for those wrongs committed when ego-driven emotions overrule their purer intentions.

The message of the book of Jeremiah can be seen as parallel to a statement about the emotional nature of a person put forth by the Edgar Cayce. He said that one should lead their life in the same manner as a Chopin nocturne. A nocturne is night music, and the nocturnes Chopin wrote have been described as languid and melancholy. The book of Jeremiah, which deals with the human emotional nature describes such a calm, reflective, and controlled state. This isn't easy as Chopin nocturnes aren't necessarily simple, but while sometimes very complex, they always have integrity and beauty.

Following Jeremiah, there is a prophecy written by the same author which is called Lamentations. It is also concerned with human emotions. Like its predecessor, it is about becoming aware that all people function through unreliable human emotions, and so one must monitor them continually. This book is about the price a person must pay when they haven't exercised self-analysis when they should. Lamentations starts with images of the holy places of Judah and Jerusalem after residents of those places attempted to resist invasion by Babylon, a nation which has been seen to be symbolic of the ego, or self-awareness. The holy nation and city had been laid waste and there was compete desolation. This is the condition of person when they persist in thinking that they are naturally pure, and so don't have to continually monitor their motivations. This portrayal of the holy city pictures the young and old lying in the streets and virgins and young men fallen by the sword. This represents the condition of a person when they resist self-examination of their natural emotions. Then nothing new or old is productive, and there is no hope for the future.

The prophet acted as an intercessor then and said, "Through the mercies of the Lord we are not consumed, because his compassions fail not." This illustrates the faith that is needed for recovery when one has avoided acknowledgement of one's naturally decadent emotional nature. The last verses of this book describe the situation where one becomes conscious of their naturally decadent, emotional nature. It is said that then "…everything we thought we had has been turned over to aliens, we have become orphans and fatherless, and slaves rule over us and we have no free hands." This describes a person with an uncontrolled emotional nature. In addition it is also said that,

"… joy has gone from our hearts, and our dancing has been turned to mourning". The Lamentations of Jeremiah ends with an explanation of the reason for this continual mourning - to bring out the truth about uncontrolled natural human emotions. It is said in the last statement of the prophecy that, "You, O Lord, reign forever; your throne endures from generation to generation." In this is the hope for ascendance to the level of the seventh chakra, which can only be achieved in the emotional domain by first mourning, having humility, and repenting from natural, carnal, emotional tendencies.

Ezekiel (God Strengthens) Physical Strength

Ezekiel wrote his prophecy while a prisoner in Babylon, an exile from Judah and the holy city of Jerusalem. Babylon, a rich and powerful nation, has been seen to represent the ego, or attribute of personal self-awareness and Jerusalem is a symbol of a place in the psyche which is ordained to be pure. This then is a prophecy that should make one aware that all people are naturally exiles from a place of purity and so they must function through awareness of their natural weakness. Ezekiel began this prophecy in the fifth year of exile in Babylon and five in Biblical mathematics is the number of grace.[21] Grace, or unmerited favor, is the only true source of strength for a person who is naturally corrupt.

Ezekiel first recorded a vision of the glory of God. It was in the form of a cloud with a continually flashing fire and in its midst glowing amber metal. Out of it came the likenesses of four living creatures with wings like angels. These creatures had men's faces and the ability to move in any direction through the use of wheels. This is a reference to the four lower chakras which are known as wheels of spiritual energy. Inherent in this is the awareness that a person can only conceive of God's reflected glory and not His essence. On earth, which is symbolized by the number four in Biblical mathematics, one may only have a faint impression of God's glory.

Ezekiel was first addressed by a voice from the midst of the vision and told that he was being sent to the chosen people, two nations which had rebelled against their destiny. The two kingdoms, Judah, and the northern kingdom, were ordained to be pure, examples to the whole world, and yet they were not functioning in this way. The prophet was warned in the vision that those to whom he was being sent were impudent and hard of heart and would not change easily. He was also told that the word of his prophecy would be railled against. This represents the attitude of a person when they become aware of their impurity and subsequent lack of strength as it's not easy to humble oneself so as to change this. There is no agreement among Bible commentators about how the prophet could see and prophesize to the chosen people and about the chosen people when he was in Babylon, but it is generally thought to have been in a dream state.

In the vision the prophet was given a scroll to eat containing words of lamentation, mourning, and woe. From this it can be seen that a person must first experience trials in order to be strengthened. The three parts of the words on the scroll likely represent the triune nature of man, symbolizing spiritual lamentation, psychic mourning, and physical woe. After eating the scroll, Ezekiel was told that he was not being sent to a people of a strange language, but to the house of Israel, the ones chosen and able to understand his message. For a person this means that anybody can be one of the chosen ones if they opt to be such, and elements of Ezekiel's message are not beyond the comprehension of anyone who might want greater physical, mental, and spiritual strength.

The voice said that eating the scroll would give great strength and endurance, as the forehead of the prophet would be made like flint in conveying the message. The seventh, or highest chakra of a person is related to a gland in their forehead and so this means that this strengthening occurs through the highest spiritual center. The psychic, Edgar Cayce, has said that the seventh chakra is concerned with spiritual healing and purity and it can strengthen the entire person, spiritually, mentally, and physically. For a person the four creatures in the fiery vision represent the lower chakras and they are intimately affected by what goes on in the highest one. This is the process of being made whole through the higher mind. This was verified in that seven days were decreed before the next message, something that should be seen as symbolic, instead of only a lapse of time. The prophet was told that he was responsible for conveying messages and not for their effect. This indicates that a person is only responsible for obeying messages received through the reflected glory of God as the results always follow.

After the voice instructed him, Ezekiel was given visions of Israel, Judah, Jerusalem, and the holy temple while he was in Babylon. According to the Edgar Cayce quote about the symbolic meaning of geographic places, Israel, Judah, and the holy temple should be seen, not as physical places, but as areas ordained to be pure in the human psyche. The prophet was told of the decadence of these supposedly holy places and that this was the reason for the seventy years of exile. The prophecy of Ezekiel goes on after his initial vision to elaborate on the theme of the decadence of the holy places and the reason for it. This should be seen as outlining specific areas for correction of personal proclivities which weaken a person. Changes in these though the elimination of certain impurities convey strength to a person. The prophecies about the decadence of the supposedly pure places are so extensive and complex that it would take a lifetime to completely decipher them for practical use.

The first thirty-two chapters of Ezekiel are admonitions to change certain decadent attitudes and behavior patterns which are related to the sixth chakra. Restoration to a holy condition for the chosen people is addressed starting in chapter thirty-three. This restoration is designed to convey strength to a person through purity of thought and stillness of the flesh. Chapter thirty-seven of the prophecy is about some dry bones coming to life, something which has been interpreted historically as the restoration of the nation of Israel, but which can also be seen as resurrection of the structure of consciousness at the level of the seventh chakra.

The prophecy of Ezekiel ends with a description of a new temple, a new worship, and a new land. The new temple represents residence at the level of the seventh chakra where the Word of God, with its many dimensions, is used to govern one's lower spiritual centers. The new worship is through grace, wherein a prince is the intercessor. The new land refers to a restored Israel, the nation of the chosen ones which is ordained to have divine strength through purity. This purity comes from the silence in the seventh chakra where righteousness reigns.

Daniel (God is my Judge) Governing

The last book of the major prophets, Daniel, continues the attunement of the sixth and seventh chakras by describing optimal ways to govern oneself. Historically it concerns the exile of the Jews in Babylon, a rich and powerful kingdom of the time. As Edgar Cayce has said, that nation should be seen as the personal quality of the ego, or self-awareness. Specifically this prophecy concerns four Hebrew young men, one of whom was the prophet Daniel. They had been taken as captives to Babylon, the nation which had vanquished Judah under King Nebuchadnezzar. Chapter one of Daniel was written in Hebrew, the language of God's chosen people. Then chapters two through six were written in Aramaic, the common language of the time, and chapters seven through twelve were again written in Hebrew. This gives an indication that this prophecy, like all the others, has a dual nature, and is concerned with the attunement of the sixth and seventh chakras. In this prophecy Daniel told King Nebuchadnezzar that he was, "...a king of kings..." In this Daniel indicated that the king of Babylon was ordained to be the ruler of all the known world at that time. In the first part of his prophecy Daniel wrote about incidents concerning himself and the three other young Hebrew men, and in the second part, starting in chapter seven, he wrote about world events. Both parts of the book present the same theme, how God rules in people's personal lives, and in world affairs.

The Bible scholar, J. Vernon McGee, has said that the key verse in the prophecy is Daniel 2:44 which is, "And in the days of these kings shall the God of heaven set up a kingdom, which shall never be destroyed; and the kingdom shall not be left to other people, but it shall break in pieces and consume all these kingdoms, and it shall stand forever."[22] This gives an indication of the cosmic, apocalyptic nature of the book, and the view it gives of eventual divine dominion in personal lives and in world affairs.

Functioning at the level of the sixth chakra is addressed in the first part of Daniel's prophecy where the affairs of individuals are addressed. And in the second part, the fate of nations until the God of heaven rules, is the subject, something which can be seen as activity in the seventh chakra. There are definite similarities between the two parts. In both chapters two and seven; four aspects of world dominion are addressed and then there is a fifth specified, which represents the rule of the eternal God. In chapter two, the four lower aspects are symbolized by an anthropomorphic image and in chapter seven these kingdoms are symbolized by four beasts. Both incidences of four elements have been widely interpreted as the kingdom of Babylon which ruled the world then, and the kingdoms of Persia, Greece, and Rome which were to come. A fifth kingdom, that of God, gets final and permanent dominion in both parts. In chapter seven, the first beast is like a lion, the second like a bear the third like a leopard, and the fourth exceedingly strong and terrible. After the fourth beast, supposedly representing the Roman empire, is destroyed, the kingdom is given to the people of the saints of the Most High, in an everlasting kingdom. The lesson to be learned is that true dominion comes from on high.

The first part of Daniel illustrates that even though there is a king on earth who is chosen by a higher power, that ruler is still always subject to Him. Chapter three of Daniel is the tale of the three Hebrew young men, who are exiles in Babylon. They refuse to worship the king's image and then are thrown into, and saved from, a fiery furnace. Chapter four describes Daniel interpreting a dream for King Nebuchadnezzar about world dominion. Chapter five is a scenario where the Babylonian empire is overthrown by the more righteous kingdom of the Medes and Persians. And chapter six is the well-known story of Daniel in a Lion's den. Each of these stories in the first half of the prophecy is concerned with the theme of God's dominion in man's life being greater than man's conceptions.

The second part of Daniel, which addresses the seventh spiritual center of man, is concerned with events which impact world systems. There are prophecies about the three kingdoms which were to follow the Babylonian, and beyond that to the coming of the messiah and his eternal rule. Mathematicians and scholars have computed the date of Jesus' coming into Jerusalem on Palm Sunday, according to a prophecy of Daniel in chapter nine. During the time Daniel was in Babylon he received messages which were said to be sealed up, something which means that they were pre-ordained and inevitable. The book of Daniel ends with the statement that these prophecies concern events that will be until the "...end of days", something which means until time as we know it is no more.   In this sense the seventh chakra is concerned with a person's relationship to eternal dominion while at the level of the sixth center, the concern is personal ruling.

Chapter Six - The Minor Prophets

After the four books of the major prophets, there are twelve books called the minor prophets. The number twelve generally symbolizes a continuous circular process, such as the twelve hours in a day or the twelve months of the year. It will be proposed that these twelve books have such a pattern, and their place in the sequence is meaningful. The following chart gives their historical sequence.

The Minor Prophets in History (B.C.E.)

1	2	3	4	5	6
Hosea	Joel	Amos	Obadiah	Jonah	Micah
750	600	750	580	800	740

7	8	9	10	11	12
Nahum	Habakkuk	Zephaniah	Haggai	Zechariah	Malachi
660	600	630	520	520	400

It is obvious that the books of the minor prophets are not in any historical sequence, and so there must be some other ordering principle. When a detailed analysis is undertaken, a pattern may be seen which is not time-dependent. This pattern appears to be a circular one which mirrors human psychological aspects. The way in which a person's mental proclivities vary has been roughly defined by psychologists and it is proposed that this is the pattern which appears in the minor prophets. This pattern reflects how a person's focus and affections continually vary. A person may be peaceful at one moment, later be dedicated to an objective, and even later be in a purely altruistic state of mind. This system of behavior which may be seen in the books of the minor prophets is reflected in a circular image known as a mandala. Psychologist Dr. Carol S. Pearson has written, "Wholeness in the psyche is traditionally symbolized by a sacred circle that is inherently harmonious because it is a microcosm of the universe." Dr. Carl Jung has described how patients approaching wholeness spontaneously drew mandalas. He said that in Sanskrit, mandala means "magic circle".[23]   Eastern religions meditate on mandalas which create specific states of awareness that foster spiritual growth.

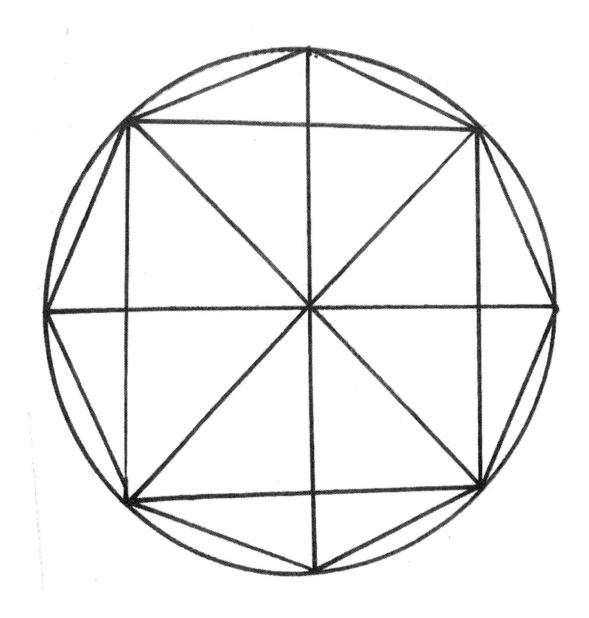

Minor Prophets Personal Attributes

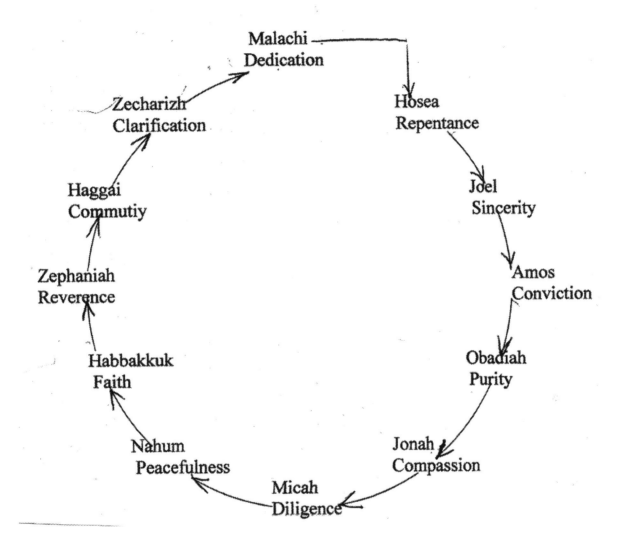

Nurturers like Dr. Pearson are currently using circular patterns of archetypes or universal images to help people focus their minds and become more functional.

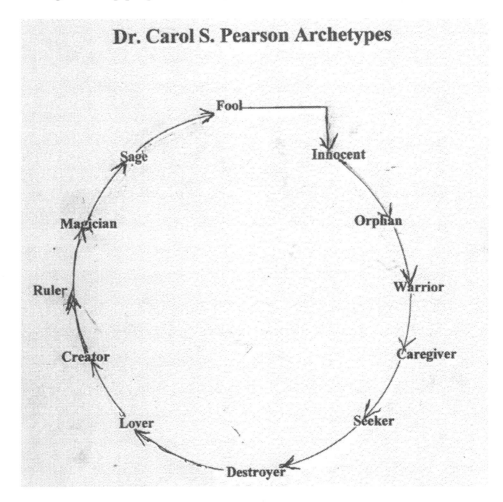

Dr. Carol S. Pearson Archetypes

Dr. Pearson is a Jungian analyst and therefore she uses the system devised by Dr. Carl Jung as the basis for her analysis of personality development. Dr. Jung used a system which saw a functional person progressing from being ego-driven to being driven by the concerns of the self. He defined the self as a personality built around concern for the center, or the universal Christ. He called this process of development "individuation", something close to that which is called salvation in standard Christianity. Dr. Pearson uses some of the same terms in her system, her description of the journey is in twelve stages, from being ego-driven to ruling one's activities through the self.

The twelve steps in the journey of a person's life in Dr. Pearson's system have been defined as the trip all must make. The journey Dr. Pearson describes starts in infancy. She calls the first step of development the archetype of the Innocent. This is where the new-born is one with their mother. At this stage, the mother will say such things as, "Let's drink our milk", assuming that there is only one entity. This lasts until the time for the child to assume a separate personality, in their first years of life. Dr. Pearson calls this next step the Orphan, the time when the person is forced to develop their own ego, or self-image. This is somewhat traumatic, and so at the next stage a person becomes a Warrior, fighting for their survival as a separate entity. Next a person sees that fighting for survival is not always beneficial and so they also become a Caregiver. These are the four steps in Dr. Pearson's system which develop the Ego. Contrary to some systems of analysis, Dr . Person's doesn't see the ego as all bad, but something to be modified into something greater.

When a person sees that they cannot survive on their own, this is the beginning of what Dr. Pearson calls Soul development. There are also four stages to this phase. They are; Seeker, Destroyer, Lover, and Creator. As with the other phases of personality development, one stage leads to another. And, as in all other phases of development, there may be shifting to other behavior archetypes on a regular basis. Some aspects of this have been called functioning through the "inner child".

The third phase of personality development in Dr. Pearson's scheme is called the Self. This phase is characterized by kingdom principles, and in her book, "Awakening the Hero Within", she illustrates this stage with stories about the mythical kingdom of Camelot. She also relates this stage to the Christian religion. In this she effectively uses stories related to the quest for the Holy Grail. The defining archetype in this phase is the Ruler, the king persona which enables one to have control of their destiny. Dr. Pearson likens this image to King Arthur who ruled the knights of the round table, another incidence of a mandala. It is significant that records of the Arthurian reign say that there were twelve knights of the round table.

A Ruler exercises dominion over the other archetypes. After a person has developed the various archetypes, they can function in such a way that they can call on any of them in given situations. And while they function as a Ruler they also use the other three archetypes in the phase, the last one, called the Self. These are Magician, Sage, and Fool. In her books, Dr. Pearson gives information which a person can use to test at what stage they might be functioning. She also gives a person help in determining if they are using shadow (negative) versions of a given archetype. By using this system, which is an expansion of the simpler system she used in her first book, "The Hero Within", she has helped many people overcome personal problems, which occur when they function in a negative manner, or through using one phase of development to the exclusion of others. In this way there is a assistance for a person in becoming whole.

The books of the minor prophets may be looked upon in the same manner as those in Dr. Pearson's system. It is possible, with intensive study of the twelve books of prophecy, to discern a personality aspect in each one. The proposed pattern of these books and their aspects is as follows.

This deciphering of the guiding mental aspects of the minor prophets is aided by the quote by Edgar Cayce that physical places have symbolic meanings. The books of the minor prophets deal largely with such ancient place names such as Judah, Israel, Babylon, Assyria, and Egypt. These are not to be truly seen as geo-political entities, but rather as psychological aspects which are like the archetypes of Dr. Pearson. By deciphering the prophetic books through using these tools , a system of naturally occurring human psychological patterns may be seen. While Dr. Pearson's system is a tool for improving human behavior, seeing a system similar to it in the minor prophets expands upon it and gives it validation. Since the Bible is considered to be divinely inspired and therefore reliable, it lends credence to a circular system of twelve archetypes. The books of the minor prophets can be seen to affect a person's behavior in a continuous circular pattern by raising energy in the ethereal body from the sixth to the seventh center in a sequential manner. However, as has been proposed by Dr. Pearson, a person may choose their guiding behavioral archetype at any given moment.

Changing one's behavior is not simple. This can be seen in people where the elimination of one destructive trait leads to another as bad or worse. However, when it is seen that behavior patterns function in a circular system, this can be avoided. It is no accident that Alcoholics Anonymous has a twelve step system as twelve is the number of a continuous process. The unique success of AA can be attributed to creating a whole person instead of just eliminating one negative behavioral habit.

There is a Hindu Upanishad which describes a rider sitting serene and motionless in his chariot which is being pulled by wild horses. Having delegated responsibility for the journey to a competent charioteer, he is free to sit back and give full attention to the passing landscape. In this story the chariot represents the body and the road over which it travels are sense objects. The horses that pull the chariot are said to be the motive forces of a person. They are wild, but having given the reins over to the hands of a competent charioteer, a person can merely enjoy the journey. This describes the method by which the twelve books of the minor prophets and twelve archetypes of Dr. Pearson are to be used. When a person uses these tools to be more functional, he is on the way to achieving what is known in Hebrew as shalom. While this term has been interpreted as "peace", it is more than that, it is a concept of completed peace with no possibility of regression.

When conceiving of a circular system of behavior, it isn't out of reason to see the halo pictured around the heads of saints and holy persons as a form of this. If a person could be of such a pure nature that they have no defects in their guiding mental archetypes, this could be reflected by an image above their head as shown in the following image.

Having stated the case for a person's guiding mental models being in a circular system of twelve archetypes, it is useful to examine a similar system in the books of the minor prophets. In this process it is well to keep in mind that all of a person's life experiences are contained in the chakras of their higher energy bodies. It is also important to realize that nations and cities in the prophetic books are to be seen as psychological aspects.

As has been proposed, in each of the twelve prophetic books, the first part describes functioning at the level of the sixth chakra and the second part functioning through the seventh spiritual center. For each prophetic book there is an English version of the name for it which comes from the Hebrew, and a personal attribute of the book.

Hosea (Salvation)   Repentance

The first book of the minor prophets, Hosea, logically follows Daniel, which was about principles of dominion in personal matters and in the world. After realizing that one has to function under a system of rules, there must be an effort to be faithful to them. This is done through continuing repentance and changes in one's behavior. Hosea was told by God to marry an unfaithful woman as an example of the northern kingdom of Israel's unfaithfulness. Hosea's wife may be seen as the adulterous nature of a person at the level of the sixth chakra. The northern kingdom was created when ten of Israel's original twelve tribes split off from the rest of the nation after deciding that following a king was too demanding. This rebellion represents a person's natural reaction to enlightened leadership. As Hosea could not change his unfaithful wife, God could not change the northern kingdom, and He cannot change a person's nature which is naturally adulterous. Only repentance and following enlightened leadership can effect a beneficial change in a person's attitudes and behavior.

Hosea wrote, "My people perish for a lack of knowledge." What is lacking is knowledge of one's tendency to fight against positive change in their nature. Such knowledge and correction is painful, but without it there would be no progress in salvation or as Dr. Jung calls it, in individuation. In this regard the people who act most foolishly are those who forget that they are naturally foolish. Edgar Cayce has said that a person's conscience is the same as their consciousness, and a person's highest consciousness is at the level of their highest spiritual centers. Hosea's wife was an adulteress and she gave birth to three children, each of whom had a name connoting corrupt qualities. Any time three elements are grouped in scripture, it is a reference to the triune nature of mankind. From this it can be seen that a person's rebellion against enlightened behavior, their adultery, results in corruption of the body, soul, and spirit. The fourteen chapters of Hosea illustrate the development of true repentance from this nature. Attempts at change come after a person perceives their unfaithfulness to ideals, and yet natural repentance is itself impure. A significant passage in Hosea relates how Jacob was a devious conniver even in his mother's womb. Jacob, whose name means "deceiver", represents basic reasoning power. This attribute is represented in the prophecy by the worship of Baals, the gods of the natural man.

The primary problem in initiating change is that natural repentance is empowering and produces a self-righteous attitude. This is seen in Hosea in the many references to

Ephriam, a name which means, "fruitfulness", and is synonymous with the northern kingdom of Israel. The associated symbolism is that when erroneous personal qualities are seen and a person's conscience is stirred, change is attempted, but self-righteousness is the only result. Pride aborts the refining process. It must become apparent to the northern kingdom, and to the naturally adulterous person that they don't have the power to change themselves. This is seen where the prophet said, "Come, let us return to the Lord after two days." Seeing that this would be the third day and three symbolizes the spirit in God and man, it becomes apparent that for repentance to be effective it must be through the spiritual centers and not through physical means or one's raw will power.

In chapter seven Hosea said that every time the Lord would heal Israel, Ephriam's guilt would be uncovered. As Israel represents the chosen people and Ephriam represents fruitfulness, the meaning of this is that every time a person repents because of knowledge of imperfections, their self-image is enhanced, something which impairs progress in salvation. This is seen in Hosea 7:1, which is, "Ephriam also is like a silly dove without heart or understanding…" This illustrates the situation where natural repentance generates a warm and fuzzy feeling and no real change. The rest of chapter seven of Hosea develops the theme of a person agonizing in repentance, something which represents the awareness that one's efforts at change can only result in self-righteousness. This is also seen in chapter eight where it is said that the wind is sown and the whirlwind is reaped. For a person this means that the wind of repentance tends to make one over-react and generate a useless whirlwind of attitudes and unimproved behavior.

Hosea continues his prophecy against carnal repentance in chapter nine where he says that they shall not remain in the Lord's land, but Ephriam shall return to Egypt and Assyria. Ephriam symbolizes fruitfulness, Egypt symbolizes the flesh, and Assyria represents excessive fervor, and so the meaning of this is that the result of a person's attempts to repent through their own power is only carnality and meaningless activity. The prophecy then mentions Assyria being in terror because of a golden calf, a symbol of idolatry. The meaning of this is that natural repentance must be refined through awareness of a person's tendency to let attempts at change become idolatrous. Then in chapter eleven Hosea said that Israel was the Lord's child when he called his son out of Egypt. The meaning of this for a person is that the son, who symbolizes the fruit of a person's efforts, is destined to be called out of carnal efforts, or Egypt.

In chapter eleven there is the most complex symbolism in the prophecy. It involves Ephriam, the symbol for fruitfulness, and Assyria a nation which represents excessive fervor. The result of this interplay is a view of functional repentance. Chapter twelve further illustrates the refinement of the repentance dynamic where it is said that Ephriam is feeding on the wind and increasing in violence, a symbol of self-righteous repentance. The conniver, Jacob, is also mentioned as being in the refining process, something which represents the reasoning function coming into play.

In chapter thirteen, a summation of Hosea's prophecy is given. This indicates that Ephriam, the fruit of repentance, was righteous when he spoke with trembling but offended when he worshiped Baal. This indicates the difference between Godly and idolatrous repentance. Finally, chapter fourteen of Hosea puts forth the methodology which can purify the adulterous northern kingdom, and the basically adulterous person. A demand is made here to return to the Lord after realizing futility of trying to use willpower to have a sincerely repentant heart. This consists of humble heeding of the words of the Lord. It is indicated in this that Assyria, symbolic of excessive fervor, cannot by herself produce constructive change. And there must also be faithfulness and awareness of specific areas for improvement that are spelled out in the word of God. When this functionality is used, the Lord is the source and real benefits may accrue. The prophecy of Hosea ends with Ephriam realizing that idolatry is not the way to make the road of salvation viable. Like the other Biblical prophecies this one ends on a high note, symbolic of driving benefits at the level of the seventh chakra.

Joel (Yahweh is God) Sincerity

The prophecy of Joel can be seen as the next step in the cycle of psychological archetypes after repentance, which was the concern of Hosea. Hosea's prophecy ended with a condition of abundance where it was said that Ephriam would have no more idols, meaning that a degree of true repentance had been achieved. Now, in a time of apparent fruitfulness, distress appears. It comes from natural forces (four types of plagues) and a political threat. The plagues are from caterpillars, locusts, creeping locusts, and cockroaches and the outside threat is the north, which is likely Assyria. The four types of plagues are meaningful in that four is the number of the world in Biblical mathematics. From this it may be seen that the purity of purpose achieved in Hosea will be tested in the world under great duress. This testing should be seen as the Lord's doing as it occurs during what is known as the day of the Lord, a time called, "A day of darkness and gloominess, a day of clouds and thick darkness".

Joel responded to the plagues by exhorting Israel to wake up as a drunkard might come to life, indicating that the warm and fuzzy state that results from being humbly repentant, as in Hosea, isn't the end of the story. Everyone can testify that when trying to improve one's behavior everything in the world seems to conspire to defeat the attempt. The negative forces which conspired against the chosen people in Joel are illustrated by images such as the vines being laid waste, fig trees ruined, new wine being dried up, and oil failing. Other pictures of a person's natural weakness in the world are the drying up of the pomegranate, the palm, and the apple tree. This illustrates that reliance on the world for personal improvement can only result in futility. The reason for this is presented next, to prepare one for the day of the Lord. This will be a time when there can only be reliance on spiritual resources. Joel said that the trumpet should be blown in Zion, indicating that the chosen people should become aware that there will be a time of final testing. The day of the Lord is a time of enforced purification, symbolized by fire. It is also a time of the testing of swift responses, represented by horse cavalry. It is said that they will rush on the cities and run on the walls, meaning that group bonds will be tested, and psychological defenses judged.

The invasion of Assyria should be seen in personal terms as the testing of the ability of a person to rise above the level of the carnal "monkey mind". And the four types of plagues should be seen in psychological terms as the testing of a person's sincerity in their progress in salvation or individuation. The purpose of this testing is to use mortification as the way to survive the day of the Lord, something described in the prophecy as being abjectly humble. This is because survival in the day of the Lord can't be done through will power, there must also be acceptance of help in the acknowledging of one's destiny. The day of the Lord demands waiting for his grace, returning to the Lord with humility and fasting. It is said that those who call on the mercy of the Lord will escape in the day of judgment.

The turning point in the prophecy of Joel is in chapter two, verse eighteen, where it is said that the Lord was jealous for his land and had pity on his people. Here the time of testing is over and those who have humbled themselves and sought mercy are considered to be the Lord's people. The rewards of this are then spelled out. They are grain, grape juice, and oil, those things symbolizing physical, relational, and spiritual benefits, as three elements in scripture are always a reference to the triune nature of man

Then it is said that the Lord would remove the northern army. This is Assyria, the country north of Israel, and for a person it represents the carnal "monkey mind". It being eliminated means that a person who survives judgment in the day of the Lord will be in a position of quiet strength at the level of the highest spiritual center. It is also decreed that the Lord would restore the years that the locusts had eaten. This represents a situation where there are no self-recriminations after becoming truly sincere. Then it is said that the Lord would pour out his spirit on all flesh, meaning that spiritual gifts would be given. Progress in salvation was prophesied for all who might call on the name of the Lord. And it is indicated that those who would survive purification would be able to pass on its benefits to others. They would have assured victory and be on the offensive, as indicated by the statement that they would, "…beat their plows into swords and their pruning hooks into spears." This is where sincerity of purpose has been achieved. It is said that then Jerusalem would be holy and Egypt and Edom desolate. This is a state of completion as Jerusalem is representative of the holy center of the persona. Egypt symbolizes the flesh state, and Edom represents regression. This state of purity of purpose is to be anticipated with joy, its nature being such that Joel says Judah would remain forever. Judah is the nation which was God-ordained to be pure. This then is a look at ascendance to the level of the seventh chakra, something which requires complete sincerity of purpose on the road of salvation.

Amos (Burden Bearer)   (Conviction of specific errors)

Historically, Amos was a lowly shepherd who condemned the upper class of Israel, the northern kingdom, during a period of prosperity. Psychologically the book of Amos addresses personal habit patterns which are thought to be optimal when they are not. This is known as conviction in some religions, becoming convinced that one has erroneous behavior patterns (sin) in their life. After the achievement of sincerity in the previous book of Joel, a person can honestly look at their life and address these issues. As in other prophecies, the naturally impure northern kingdom can be regarded as functioning through the sixth chakra, where there is pride instead of the acceptance of grace.

Amos started with a condemnation of six geo-political areas surrounding Israel: Damascus, Gaza, Tyre, Edom, Amon, and Moab. Then there are condemnations of the chosen people of Judah and Israel. All these condemnations are in the form of, "For three transgressions, and for four…" This likely means that the erroneous behavior patterns are so entrenched that nothing can withhold condemnation of them. These are deviant habits that can be established in a person and must be made known to them in no uncertain way.

Summary of the Condemnations in Amos

Guilty	Condemnation	Deviant Habit Pattern
Geo-political area		

Damascus (Assyrians)	Threshed Gilead	Excessive egoistic fervor which impairs wellness
Gaza (Philistines)	Enslaved the Jews	Worldliness which impairs purity
Tyre (Traders)	Overcame Edom	Greed which impairs natural produce
Edom (Offspring of Esau)	Corrupted Jacob	Impurity which dilutes piety
Ammon (Offspring of Lot)	Aborted Gilead	Impurity which impairs natural goodness
Moab (Offspring of Lot)	Ruined Edom	Egotism which impairs faith
Judah	Despised the Law and has not kept His commandments	Knowing correct behavior and yet not doing it
Israel	Was covetous, unfaithful, abused the poor, sexually impure, used false piety	Being one of the chosen ones and yet using carnal behavior

The first condemnation was of Damascus, which was the capitol of Assyria, and as such a symbol of the carnal mind. It was condemned because it had threshed Gilead, which was the area east of the Jordan River where two and a half tribes of Israel had settled. It was a secure area and as such a symbol of natural prosperity. When it was said that Damascus threshed it, this indicates a tendency for a person to destroy natural prosperity through excessive fervor, even through such means as a valid religious system. The second condemnation was of Gaza, which was the home of the Philistines, a godless, itinerant, sea-faring people. The condemnation was that they had made slaves of the Jews, the chosen people. In a person this symbolizes a pattern where their natural inclinations hinder their higher nature.

The third condemnation was of Tyre, a rich trading city on the Mediterranean. It was condemned for its treatment of Edom, a city founded by the offspring of Esau, the untamed brother of Jacob. This is a condemnation of the tendency for a person to prefer immediate gain over the produce of nature. Then, in the fourth condemnation, Amos condemned Edom for its treatment of Jacob, who is a symbol of the nation of Israel. This was a condemnation of the pattern where a person uses suspect motives in place of more refined or spiritual goals. Next there was a condemnation of Amon, which was also founded by the offspring of a relationship between Lot and one of his daughters. This relationship was necessary so that there would be no pagan descendents of Abraham, the father of faith It was said that Amon ripped up women with children in Gilead. This represents the tendency for a person to allow a small amount of faith to impair natural fruitfulness. The sixth prophecy condemned Moab, saying that it had burned the bones of the king of Edom. Edom has the same symbolism here as before, children of the chosen people, and Moab is a symbol of impure faith as it was founded by one of the offspring of an incestuous relationship between Lot and one of his daughters. This then symbolizes the tendency for a person to allow impure faith to eliminate ruling through natural law. Amos himself was a shepherd, a man of the fields, so his voice is one of the common sensibility needed for purification of vagrant habit patterns.

Next in Amos come images which address areas of deficiencies in the people of the northern and southern kingdoms, those ordained to be pure. This means that in analyzing one's habit patterns, one should be open to correction even when they seem to spring from pure motives. The two kingdoms of the chosen people symbolize the purest areas in a person's psyche as they were descended from the father of faith, Abraham, and had the laws of Moses.

All the deficiencies to be conscious of in Amos involve situations where the rich oppress the poor, and the strong lord it over the weak. For a person, this means that one should examine their habitual tendencies where they think they are always correct. A concept used to make this clear is the plumb line, a tool used to measure the relation of a structure to the earth with precision. Using a personal plumb line consists of seeing that all was created by the Lord, and He has set standards that are for each person's benefit.

The prophecies in Amos should be seen as condemnations of behavior where a person might be pleased with themselves, instead of humbly seeking the real truth. To reinforce this an image is presented of the "cows of Bashan", something which can be interpreted as the tendency towards lethargy and self-satisfaction. Amos put forth the concept that there once was poverty and deficiency in the kingdoms of the chosen people, but the grace of the Lord caused prosperity, and yet there is no acknowledgement of this. This is where a person has had their energy system raised from the lower levels, but isn't functioning in humble gratefulness so that greater refinements can take place.

As with the other prophecies in the Old Testament, the book of Amos has two distinct parts. The first part is a revelation of habitual faults which is similar to activity at the level of the sixth chakra. The latter part is like activity in the seventh chakra which starts in Amos 9:11. Here the fortunes of the kingdoms of Judah and Israel are restored which symbolizes impure personal tendencies having been accounted for. Because of this hope is given then that the chosen people can remain in the holy land to which they were destined. For a person this is functioning at the level of the seventh spiritual center in evaluating personal tendencies and behavior patterns.

Obadiah (Servant of Yahweh) Purity

Historically, the book Obadiah is a prophecy that Israel would eliminate Edom, a nation founded by the descendents of Esau, the twin brother of Jacob. Jacob was refined and sensitive, while Esau was wild and untamed. The source of Esau's grossness can be seen where it is said that the pride of Edom's heart had been a source of deception, there has been

"…soaring in him like an eagle and a nest among the stars." This is a reference to the pride which promotes untamed behavior. This prophecy logically follows Amos, a book which contains information about how a person truly functions, something which can make one proud.

Obadiah pronounced judgment on Edom because of it's gloating over temporary ascendance over Jacob, a name synonymous with Israel, the nation of the chosen ones. Verse five of the only chapter of the prophecy condemns the thievery of Edom, which means that the grosser side of a person has been stealing from the more refined. This has been caused by a lack of knowledge about Esau, meaning that there was ignorance about the baser side of human nature. This prophecy then is about overcoming one's evil twin, their grosser tendencies. Verse ten describes the times in history when Edom joined with foreign power in wars that captured Jerusalem. For a person this is a description of the times when egotism and grossness allowed impure tendencies to gain the upper hand over pure attitudes and behavior. It is implied that this happened when the more refined brother had met with misfortune. This represents times in a person's life when they might have sincerely tried to use knowledge to behave correctly and yet didn't seem to be rewarded.

For a person, the book of Obadiah should be seen as a condemnation of using knowledge in the wrong manner. The psychic, Edgar Cayce, has put forth a principle concerning this. He has said that all gains in knowledge must be accompanied by an increase in humility. In observing this one can see that addictive behavior generally results from having knowledge without character. Addictions come from an inaccurate view of human nature as it was optimally designed, which is to be intelligent and yet humble. This is seen in Obadiah where the final the elimination of the nation whose source was the egoistic Esau is prophesized. When this has been accomplished, purity of character is enhanced and the tendency toward self-gratification is ameliorated. This represents functioning at the level of the seventh charka concerning these matters.

Jonah (The Dove) Compassion

The prophecy of Jonah comes after that of Obadiah, whose purpose was to enhance purity of character in a person. This is a logical sequence as Jonah is concerned with achieving a compassionate nature and it can often be seen that a pure person is not necessarily a compassionate one. The well-known book of Jonah conforms to the pattern of addressing the sixth and seventh charkas, as it is in two parts. The first part is before the prophet was swallowed by a great fish, and the second after he was disgorged on land. Historically Jonah was called to prophesy against Nineveh, the capitol of ancient Assyria. That nation was known to be completely ruthless, and as such, can be seen as that tendency in a person. A certain amount of ego-driven fervor is not completely negative at lower levels of functioning, but it is not something that is functional at more refined levels.

Historically Jonah was sent by God to preach repentance to Nineveh, but knowing the nature of the people there, he went in the opposite direction. This represents the behavior of a person when they don't have enough dedication to counter egoistic fervor. After going away from Nineveh on a ship, the sailors found Jonah to be the cause of a great storm and they cast him into the sea. There he was swallowed by a "great fish". The defining moment for Jonah came when he was in the fish and repented of avoiding his destiny. He said, "When my heart fainted within me, I remembered the Lord and my prayer came in unto thee, into thine holy temple." This represents the realization that a person has no choice but to fulfill their destiny and resist selfishness.

Jonah then obediently went on a three-day journey to Nineveh where he prophesied about the God of Israel. Three in Biblical mathematics represents resurrection, divine completion, and perfection.[24] This means that Jonah allowed himself to be resurrected into a form which enabled him to deny egoistic fervor at the levels of the body, mind, and spirit. He preached that there were forty days until Nineveh would be destroyed if there wasn't repentance and forty is the number of testing and trials in Biblical mathematics.[25] The meaning of this for a person is that after realizing the necessity for resisting ruthless personal tendencies, there is a time of testing of their ability to do so.

The final vignette in the prophecy came when Jonah was angry that he had preached repentance to his ruthless enemies and they were granted pardon. He said that this was why he had fled in the opposite direction in the first place – he knew that God was compassionate and would change His mind about destroying His enemies. The sun then shone strongly on the prophet, and God was compassionate and provided a gourd plant to give him shade, although later a worm ate it. Jonah was told that this was the same quality that had been manifested in him through his prophecy against the ruthless Assyrians. Compassion was the quality that changed the people of Nineveh and it is the quality which can enable a person to resist egoistic fervor. This enables a person to function at the level of the seventh charka in this regard.

Micah (Who is Like Yahweh)   Diligence

This prophecy is a condemnation of self-satisfaction in a person. After the book of Jonah, which portrayed modification of excessive fervor, there is a tendency towards lethargy and self-satisfaction, something which is to be eliminated here. Historically Micah's prophecy was directed against Samaria and Jerusalem, the capital cities of Israel and Judah. When excessive fervor has ceased driving a person, as occurred in Jonah, there is a lack of dynamism which results in a lack of diligence in governing. In Micah 1:3, the prophet said that the Lord would come down and tread on the high places. These high places are egoistic estimates of one's ability to rule their affairs without exercising effort. The issue of graven images and idols was addressed next. This refers to smug complacency, to a person not making hard choices and eliminating sacred cows. Chapter two continues this theme with a condemnation of working evil on one's bed, another image of smug self-satisfaction. Wine and strong drink are condemned here also, a commentary on a lack of humble effort at this point in personal development.

Chapter four of Micah is a description of the eventual reward for humble steadfastness. The latter days are described as the mountain of the Lord being established, all peoples flowing to it, and the Lord teaching there. This is the part of Micah where the chosen people are promised eventual victory. There is such a striking difference between the two parts of the prophecy that scholars have commented that there might have been two authors of it.[26]

The perseverance required to be one of the Lord's people is described here in such phrases as, "Be in pain and labor to bring forth, O daughter of Zion, like a woman in travail..." The way to combat complacency is seen in this as being humble and dedicated.

This is illustrated by a description of the insignificant city of Bethlehem as ordained to be the birthplace of the ruler from everlasting to everlasting. With him leading the way one is exhorted to, "Arise, contend thou before the mountains, and let the hills hear thy voice." Mountains in scripture are symbolic of people groups, so this is an exhortation for the chosen people to stand up to temptations from the world's system which would impair their dedication.

The attitude that eliminates graven images and idols is then described by the phrase, "Do justly, love mercy, and walk humbly before thy God." The snare of egoistic complacency is pictured in the statement, "For the rich men thereof are full of violence, and the inhabitants thereof have spoken lies, and their tongue is deceitful in their mouth." It is to be realized from this that anyone who thinks they are virtuous simply because they have eliminated excessive fervor, is mistaken and they will fall into the trap of egoistic complacency. Chapter seven of Micah continues the condemnation of complacently relying on anthropomorphic motivations where it is written, "Woe is me! For there is no cluster to eat; my soul desired the first-ripe fruit." Again it is said that, "The best of them is as a briar; the most upright is sharper than a thorn hedge…" This brings into focus the battle against relying on vain human efforts. There are also admonitions not to trust a friend or family member, representing a potential lack of dynamism in familiar relationships. Then it is said that one should bear the indignation of the Lord and show Him homage.

Micah ends with the realization that the Lord pardons those who seek after Him and are not satisfied with themselves or in human relationships. The most effective way to maintain this attitude is by being ashamed of a high estimate of oneself. By humbly honoring the greatness of the Lord one becomes aware of the natural human tendency to function below the level of the highest chakra because of lethargy and complacency.

Nahum (Comfort) Peacefulness

Historically the destruction of Nineveh, the capitol city of the Assyrian empire was prophesized by Nahum. This represents the elimination of the empire which overcame the northern kingdom of Israel, the demise of the pagan nation which the Lord used to teach the chosen people a lesson. As has been seen, the Assyrians were completely ruthless, and as such, a symbol of the psychological aspect to be dealt with here. For a person the destruction of the Assyrian empire represents the elimination of the lower, carnal mind, the source of egoistic fervor.

This prophecy has been placed around 610 B.C.E., just before the fall of the Assyrian empire. It starts with a characterization of the director of world events as a jealous and avenging God. This idea is expanded upon with the theme that there exists a call to purification, a day of the Lord. As the ruthless Assyrian empire existed for a long time, egoistic fervor has existed in a person throughout the purifying of their lower chakras. The reason for this is stated in Nahum 1:3; "The Lord is slow to anger, but great in power, and the Lord will by no means clear the guilty." Despite the ruthless determination of the Assyrians, the will of the Lord is infinitely greater. Undirected psychic energy has run its course, and peaceful acceptance of a more refined dynamic is decreed at this point in personal development. This is seen in the proclamation of Nahum 1:15; "Look! On the mountains, the feet of one who brings good tidings, who proclaims peace!" This peace is to be achieved by the superior power of a higher form of energy than that which was ruthless and undirected. Devastation of the devastator is prophesied as inevitable. The elimination of the merciless power which overcame the carnal Egyptians and strong Ethiopians is prophesized in Nahum.

Images of the inability of excessive egoistic energy to prevail are vividly portrayed here, showing that nothing prevails against the will of the Lord. It has been said that this is the only book of the prophets which ends on a minor note, as it concludes with the elimination of an entire people group, the Assyrians. While this might appear to be true, the peace and quiet that reign when excessive undirected psychic energy has been eliminated is truly a positive condition. This entails functioning at the level of the seventh chakra where there are unlimited resources of purity, as then one is functioning as a chosen one, doing the Lord's will. Then it can be seen that there is great gain when ruthless, carnal energy, as personified by the Assyrians, is eliminated, as it must be at this point in personal progress.

Habakkuk (Embracer)   Faithfulness

This prophecy, which largely concerns functioning through faith, logically follows Nahum, a proclamation about the elimination of egoistic fervor. This is so because without the energy that previously drove a person they can be subject to a lack of direction, something which can be overcome only by stepping into the unknown through faith. Historically this is a prophecy about the Babylonian empire overcoming Judah, and the best of the chosen people being removed to Babylon. As previously seen, Babylon is a symbol of the ego, and the southern kingdom of Judah represents the holy center of the persona. This prophecy then is about the situation where a lack of motivation towards purity results in functioning through the ego, or self-awareness.

Initially, it is said that there was violence in Judah because there wasn't any effective law or judgment. In the previous step, the book of Nahum, the elimination of excessive psychic energy was portrayed, symbolized by the destruction of the nation of Assyria. As a boat cannot sail without wind, a person cannot function without psychic energy as then there is no direction. A hint of what is needed is seen in Habakkuk 2:4 where it is said, "Behold the proud; his soul is not upright in him; but the just shall live by his faith." The prophet said that what was about to occur would be marvelous and that the heathen nations would wonder at it. This represents the situation where the holy center of personality is threatened by egotism, something which couldn't happen to baser parts of the persona, symbolized here by the "heathen". Since Judah, the holy center, is without direction and in disarray, it can be overcome by the swift and terrible power of Babylon, the nation which represents the overarching ego. The image of a net is presented, something which is a picture of the egotism into which a person can fall and become captured. If one thinks that they are in a situation of calm effectiveness through their own virtue they will revert to self-empowerment as their source of motivation.

The threat of being overcome by the ego, symbolized by invasion by Babylon, is present in the first part of Habakkuk's prophecy. To counter this it is said, "Behold, his soul which is lifted up is not upright in him; but the just shall live by faith." Then there is a description of the self-righteous that, "…he trangresseth by wine…", indicating that a person can be intoxicated by their own sense of self-worth. Habakkuk 2:9 continues this theme with, "Woe to him that coveteth an evil covetousness to his house, that he may set his nest on high, that he may be delivered from the power of evil." Anyone who thinks that they can be effective through self-empowerment will always be proven wrong.

There are many examples of what is to be realized here, which is self-absorption after the repression of natural human energy. Malignancy occurs in a person when natural energy is suppressed and another source of motivation isn't found. This may be seen in the numerous examples which indicate that the cause of cancer is the repression of natural energy. An example of this can be seen where men who get prostate cancer have usually exhibited a noticeable amount of repression of sexual energy. The same holds true for women, as breast cancer was once called, "The Nun's Disease" because of its high incidence in women who repressed their sexuality. There are similar examples of repression causing malignancy, such as the willful denial of natural creative energy causing pancreatic cancer, as the pancreas is the source of energy for the body. This principle is described in 2:13, which is, "Hath not the Lord Almighty determined that the people's labor is only fuel for the fire, that the nations exhaust themselves for nothing?"

The only valid substitute for the natural energy which was repressed in the previous step is seen in Habakkuk 2:14, which is, "For the earth will be filled with the knowledge of the glory of the Lord as the waters cover the sea." The glory of the Lord who created and is creating all that exists is the only viable substitute for natural motivations. Verse nineteen of chapter two makes the point that all one's own desires can produce are graven images. Chapter two ends with the statement, "But the Lord is in his holy temple; let all the earth keep silence before him."

Chapter three of Habakkuk is where a valid source of energy is described. It is said to be a prayer of praise which is to be set to wild, enthusiastic, and triumphal music. This is where the victories of the Lord through faith are celebrated. It is a recounting of triumphs which were gained through the terrible might of the Lord of Israel. The theme developed here is how all worldly powers are ordained to be subservient to divine will and how the chosen ones should have faith in the future because of past victories. Such events are mentioned as the pestilence on the Egyptians which led to the freedom of the Hebrews, the triumph over the Midianites in the time of the judges, and the occasion when the sun stood still in the heavens to give victory to Joshua. The recounting of the victories of the chosen people is followed by Habakkuk 3:16 which is, "I heard and my heart pounded, my lips quivered at the sound; decay crept into my bones... yet I will wait patiently for the day of calamity to come on the nation invading us." It is shown here that victory comes through waiting on the will of the Lord instead of doing that which might be ego-enhancing. This illustrates resting at the level of the seventh chakra where enlightened faith never fails.

Zephaniah (Yahweh My Secret)   Reverence

The previous book of Habakkuk was concerned with developing faith in a person and now the prophet Zephaniah shows how to use the power of belief to exercise purity of worship. Historically Zephaniah was said to be a descendent of the good king, Hezekiah, and his prophecy is a condemnation of the wickedness of the whole earth. For a person, this is a description of the way to eliminate impure motivations so as to be able to worship reverently.

Zephaniah starts with a condemnation of Judah, a nation which is an archetype of a place in a person which is ordained to be pure. First there is a declaration that idolatrous worship of Baal must stop. He said that false worship, characterized as "…worshipping heaven on housetops", must cease. This must be done because of the imminent day of the Lord, a point at which purity is imperative. The term "day" should be regarded as a dispensation and not a specific point in time. There is always allowance for slippage when attempts are made to use pure motives, but there is a limit to the extent to which one may use faith carnally. The Lord is merciful and long-suffering, and yet there is a point in a person's journey in salvation when He will demand purity. An aspect that will be judged is the trading proclivity as it is said in the prophecy that the merchant people will be condemned. For a person, this is a condemnation of trying to bargain ones way with God instead of simply seeking His will.

The day of the Lord, was seen by Zephaniah as a time of wrath, trouble, waste, and darkness. The way to survive it was then described as being meek and trying to achieve holiness through humility. Some old, natural ways have to be eliminated, symbolized by the prophesized destruction of Gaza, Askelon, Ashdod, and Canaan, all tribes of Godless people who lived by the sea near Judah. Also marked for elimination were Moab and Ammon. Those nations were near the holy land, and yet hostile to the nation of the chosen people. The Ethiopians, powerful, but pagan people, were also marked for elimination. The capital of Assyria, Nineveh, which was the seat of ruthlessness, was also specifically targeted for eradication in this regard because of it's corrupt nature. Aspects of Nineveh's nature are described in Zephaniah 3:3 as , "Her princes within her midst are roaring lions; her judges are evening wolves; they leave not a bone till morning." Assyria symbolizes egoistic fervor, and so here it symbolizes attempting to function through one's own power and not in reverent humility before a Superior Power. All impure tendencies are ordained to be replaced by reverent humility, symbolized by shepherds here.

The futility of one trying to be reverent in an assertive way is described in Zephaniah 3:7. Here the Lord declares that He told those who wanted to come close to Him that they must first fear Him, and in this they have been corrupt. The next verse describes the way to avoid the Lord's condemnation, which is to wait upon Him. Humbly waiting on the will of the Lord is the way to be judged righteous rather than blindly trying to be affirmed through one's own efforts

Zephaniah prophesized about a time when all nations would have one language, which means that all facets of the universal persona would be cooperative. It is indicated that then transgressions would be taken away as there wouldn't be the addressing of matters beyond one's ability. All people would acknowledge that they were naturally impure, and yet mercy would be afforded them. Deceitful behavior will have ceased and there would be no anxiety since there would be appreciation for the mercy afforded the humble. A time of sincere rejoicing and singing was prophesized to occur then, a dispensation when the meek would wait on the mercy of the Lord with joy. The ones sincerely sorrowing because of their inherent impurity would then be gathered into a holy assembly. This represents the raising of spiritual energy from the impure sixth charka to the silence of the seventh spiritual center by humbly waiting for help in purification. True worship would then reach a pinnacle when all contrary elements would be resolved and there would be no more pagan aggressiveness in worship through false pretense. This is said to be a time when all nations would revere the holy land and function in purity. For a person this is a time when all facets of personality would function in humble reverence, representing ascendance to the level of the seventh chakra when attempting to worship.

Haggai (Yahweh My Feast)   Intercession

This prophecy is designed to use the reverence achieved in Zephaniah to help a person function in a group manner so there can be multiplied benefits through sharing. Historically, it was an admonition for the Jews who had returned from Babylon to build a temple for group worship. It is comprised of four brief words of the Lord conveyed through the prophet Haggai in 520 B.C.E., the second year of the reign of Darius the Persian. It is meaningful that the name "Darius" means, "He who informs himself" as this is the way the prophecies under his reign should be seen, as opportunities for self-examination. At this point in history the known world was under the rule of the Persians who had overcome the Babylonians, those who had forced the Jews into exile. As has been seen, Babylon represents the ego, and up to this point in the minor prophets, one should have realized that the chosen people being in exile there represents functioning through self-empowerment. Now, under Darius' reign, something greater than that is presented. This may be seen in that the Persians, have allowed the chosen people to return to their beloved and pure homeland of Judah.

"Nelson's complete Book of Bible Maps and Charts" describes the historical situation of this prophecy as, "The destruction of Jerusalem had humbled a once-proud people, and they were influenced by the Persian view that all religions were equal in value. Therefore, the Jews did not follow rigorous religious practices, and were not concerned with rebuilding the temple."[27] This also describes the condition of a person at this stage as the previous prophecy of Zephaniah enabled a person to function in a reverent manner, but not in a group setting that would produce mutual benefits. Historically, this was a time to build a common meting place for worship so that there could be intercession, under the aegis of the priesthood.

There were four words of the Lord conveyed to the prophet. They were given to Zerubbabel, the Governor, Joshua the priest and the people who had returned from Babylon.

Words of the Lord in Haggai

Word of The Lord	Day, Month, Year of Darius' Reign	To Whom Given	Meaning of the Word
1.	1,6,2	Zerubbabel, Joshua	You do not prosper as the temple of the Lord has not been rebuilt

2	21,7,2	Zerubbabel, Joshua, the people	The temple seems small now, but it will be filled with glory
3	24,9,2	All assumed	The priesthood is for intercession, to bring purity out of uncleanness, virtue where none existed.
4	24,9,2	Zerubbabal	The Governor, Zerubbabel, is to now function as a priest also

The first word of the Lord was conveyed on the first day of the sixth month of the second year of Darius' reign. In Biblical mathematics, the number one symbolizes unity, six is the number of man, and two is the number of redoubled effect and witness.[28] The redoubled effect comes when two or more people come together in unity of purpose. The word of the Lord first came through the prophet to Zerubbabel, the governor of Judah, and Joshua, the high priest. The governor symbolizes the director of actions in a person and the priest represents intercession, where a person helps another. While this is a historical prophecy about the building of a temple for common worship, it is also a description of the process a person goes through in developing social skills which enable them to benefit a group.

This first word to the people was that although they didn't think the time had come to build a place for meeting, they weren't prospering because the Lord wasn't glorified in such a place. This message stirred Zerubbabel the governor, Joshua the high priest, and the people. There being a combination of three things, the meaning here is that common worship would bring benefits at the physical, relational, and spiritual levels. Construction of the temple was started on the twenty-fourth day of the sixth month of the second year of Darius' reign. The twenty-fourth day marking the beginning of construction indicates that group worship is to be accomplished through intercession, as this number in Biblical mathematics symbolizes the priesthood. As has been seen, the sixth month symbolizes the nature of man and the second year stands for redoubled effect.

The second word to Haggai came on the twenty-first day of the seventh month of the second year of Darius' reign. Twenty-one refers to the terribleness of sin, seven is the number of completion and two means redoubled effect in Biblical mathematics. [29] This word then is about atonement in the temple for sins the chosen people have committed. Haggai was told by the Lord to say to Zerubbabel and Joshua that anyone who had seen the first temple would say that the present one was as nothing. This means that a person considers their goodness now less grand than before when they basically only followed the law. The first temple represents functioning through obedience to established principles, a reference to the tabernacle built under the lawgiver, Moses. That was the kind of goodness that was developed in the Old Testament before the prophetic books. The second temple can be seen as the one described in Isaiah, where an intercessor, the messiah, was first seen, and it has been modified since. In Isaiah the temple was begun with an admonition to, "...reason together", meaning to alter one's simplistic mode of thinking which was based on the law. Worship in the old temple entailed functioning through certain principles as represented in the books before the prophets. The new temple has been constructed through a more refined concept, complex images or archetypes, and since then one's sense of self has been greatly altered. One's concept of their own righteousness now is not nearly as grand as it was before when there were only simple rules to follow. Now, at the levels of the sixth and seventh chakras, a person is exposed to their abject nature in relation to their Creator and their sense of self-worth isn't nearly what it was before.

The first temple, the concept of the self that previously existed, is described in Haggai 2:5 as the word which was covenanted when the people of Israel came out of Egypt. Coming out of Egypt represents leaving a carnal state, something done through the law. The new temple is being built on grace through an intercessor and it changes one's sense of themselves. Haggai then said that the heavens and the earth, the sea, and dry lands would be shaken. This means that concepts and values that were developed under creation and the law would be radically altered in the new temple, the more refined and true one built on grace through intercession. Haggai also said that all nations would be shaken, and as has been seen, nations are symbolic of psychic proclivities at the level of the sixth and seventh chakras. The glory of the latter temple was prophesized to be greater than that of the former one as it would be the final one, constructed on grace. This final state is to be based on universal goodness through gracious intercession.

The third word to Haggai came on the twenty-fourth day of the ninth month of the second year of Darius's reign. In Biblical mathematics, twenty-four is the number of the priesthood, nine is the number of the fruit of the spirit and divine completeness from the Lord, and two is still redoubled effect. [30] This prophecy then is about how the intercession of the priesthood is to bear fruit. This word told Haggai to ask the priests if one who had done unclean acts could ever be declared clean. The assumption is that the condition of a person at the level of the sixth chakra is one of incomplete holiness, although there is a beginning, as indicated by the start of construction on the new temple. Although a person may not yet be able to function in a completely pure manner, if they rely on the intercessory priesthood they can still function without guilt.

It is said in this word that a person who put in fifty measures would only draw twenty measures, a significant loss. This means that fifty measures of effort only yielded twenty measures of results through set principles of the human mind, emotions, using the body, and the ego. Because this sermon was preached in the ninth month, a number which is symbolic of the fruit of the spirit and divine completeness, the meaning is that more goodness can be achieved through intercessory grace than by only trying to follow set principles. Haggai 2:19 records that there are blessings, and yet the vine, the fig tree, the pomegranate, and the olive tree have not brought forth anything of value. This describes functioning through grace where attempts at pure behavior are made through faith alone. This indicates that there can be virtue even though a virtuous act has not been performed yet.

The fourth and final word was given by Haggai to Zerubbabel, the governor, on the twenty-fourth day of the ninth month and it was also in the second year of Darius' reign. The numbers of the day and month are significant as they again symbolize the priesthood and the fruit of the spirit. It is significant that twenty four is the number of the priesthood as there are twenty-four cranial nerves in the human head and this is where the sixth and seventh chakras interface. There is a description of the heavens and earth being shaken and the kingdoms of the heathen being overthrown. The ruling faculty in a person, symbolized here by Zerubbabel the governor, was then given notice that some associations which are products of the law are going to be changed when they might not be useful any more. Zerubbabel was also given notice that he had been chosen for a divine purpose, to rule in an intercessory or priestly manner. To secure this, the governor was told that he should be like a signet ring, something which is a symbol of the priesthood. From this point on the governor is to be a priest, an intercessor also. This will make group functioning effective through intercession for anyone who might need it. When the ruler is also the intercessor, grace is the dynamic instead of the law. This is the achievement of functioning in a community manner, through acceptance of grace at the level of the seventh chakra.

Zechariah (Yahweh Remembers) Clarifying

The purpose of this prophecy is indicted by its name, "Yahweh Remembers". It is designed to clear up confusion through summarizing what has gone before. It is basically a synopsis of the development of intercessory grace through a messiah. The number of the sequence of the books of the minor prophets relates to their functions and this is the eleventh of those books. This is the eleventh book in the cycle of the minor prophets, and that number in Biblical Mathematics which means "disorder and judgment".[31] This is because there is inevitably confusion concerning matters in the first ten of the prophetic books, and in this one disorder is addressed and clarification provided. "Nelson's Complete Book of Bible Maps and Charts" says, "Zechariah moves from gentile domination to messianic rule, from persecution to peace, and from uncleanness to holiness." [32] For a person this means creating a place in consciousness for the messiah. This is done in the most effective way, by using images instead of simple word forms, something first seen in Isaiah. This book fulfills the premise first proposed in the preface, that, as Edgar Cayce said, that the purpose of all creation is to restore the universe as we know it to a condition of wholeness, or universality. This is to be accomplished by bringing wellness to each individual person as wholeness is brought to the universe.

The first word of the Lord in Zechariah's prophecy came in the eighth month of the second year of Darius' reign. Darius was the Persian king who gave the Judeans permission to go back to their homeland from captivity in Babylon. His name means, "He who Informs

Himself", something which is meaningful when considering the minor prophets from a personal standpoint. This is a new way of functioning for a person, as indicated by the number of the month of this word, eight. That number in Biblical mathematics represents new beginnings. The two for the year in this word means redoubled power and witness.[33] In this word Zechariah said that the Lord was displeased with the fathers of this generation because they had prophets to warn them to change their evil ways and they didn't do so. This likely refers to the ten books that precede this one, prophecies whose purpose for a person was to describe the way to function through grace so that they may lead a serene and balanced life. However, since the average person isn't able to immediately assimilate everything that was said, this prophecy is designed to correct that.

The second word of the Lord to Zechariah came on the twenty-fourth day of the eleventh month of the second year of Darius' reign. In Biblical mathematics twenty-four represents the priesthood, eleven is the number of judgment, and disorder, and two means redoubled effect. The meaning of this word then is that the intercession of a priest is to be used in making judgments of right and wrong and bringing order. This word contains eight visions and that number has been seen to symbolize new beginnings. This new beginning is functioning through the grace afforded by an intercessor. The following chart illustrates these visions.

The development of Grace in Zechariah's Eight Visions

8. 4 Chariots and

2 mountains

Making grace universal

7. Woman in

a basket

Making grace absolute

6. A flying

scroll

Transmitting grace

5. Lampstand &

olive trees

Making grace automatic

4. Joshua accused,

Affirming grace

3. A Man with

measuring rod

Utilizing grace

2. 4 Horns and

4 smiths

Empowered by grace

1. Colored horses

Accepting grace

The first of the eight visions was of a rider and four colored horses. The rider was on a red horse and leading three other horses that were red, sorrel, and white. Horses in scripture are conveyers of qualities, transporters of a given dynamic, and the color red symbolizes power. Since this entire word relates to the intercessory priesthood and redoubled effect, the horseman astride the red horse and leading the three other horses likely represents an intercessor directing a person's body, soul, and spirit. This then illustrates the most basic concept of grace, a person receiving unearned virtue in all aspects of their being.

The second vision in this word was of four horns and four smiths. Horns in the Bible are symbolic of power and four is the number of the earth in Biblical Mathematics. It is said that these horns have scattered Judah, Israel, and Jerusalem. These three geopolitical places are those ordained to be pure, and the fact that there are three of them means they represent the triune aspect of mankind. The meaning of this vision then must be that earthly forces have diluted man's originally pure nature. Next, in this vision, it is said that the horns of the nations were lifted up against Judah to scatter the people. This then means that worldliness has been hampering a person's efforts at being restored to their original purity. Then an image of four smiths or carpenters was presented, and it was said that they were to cast out the horns of the nations that had scattered Judah. The four artisans represent skillfulness and so the meaning here is likely that the virtue of the intercessory priesthood is to be used to restore purity to a person.

The third vision was of a man with a rod in his hand with which he was to measure Jerusalem. Jerusalem has been seen as an archetype of a holy area in a person, a place which no power on earth or in heaven can change except a person's will. An angel said that Jerusalem would be inhabited as a town without walls or protection built by man, but that the Lord would be a wall of fire around her. This likely represents grace being used to govern a person's behavior instead of set principles. The measuring rod represents judgment, so this implies that when functioning through grace there is no need to build a wall of specific principles around intentions. Then there was an order for the chosen people to flee from the land of the north, a land which is considered by scholars to be Babylon – to flee to the four winds of heaven. Babylon, as previously seen represents the ego, so the meaning here is likely that the ego-drive in a person has to be abandoned in favor of grace when utilizing priestly intercession. Then it was said that the nations, symbolic of personal qualities, were to be tried and joined to the Lord. Nations, such as Assyria, are to be refined and joined to the holy land in a state of purity. Assyria, for example, an archetype of excessive personal fervor, can be changed into a positive force for good. And Babylon, symbolic of the raw ego drive in a person, can be refined so that it promotes the gathering of all souls into one. All the changes in these visions are to be the result of utilizing grace through the intercessory priesthood.

The fourth vision was of Joshua, the high priest, and he was accused by Satan of having filthy garments, which he indeed had. This represents a person thinking that they are hopelessly condemned for having violated at least one principle of righteousness that they have been exposed to. They are therefore subject to negativity and might think that intercession by a priest is useless. The angel of the Lord then gave an order to take away the filthy garments of the priest and to put a mitre on his head, something which represents authority. And it was then said that the Branch would be brought forth. The Branch is the righteous intercessor, and his authority is to be made available to all.

In the fifth vision of the second word an angel came to Zechariah and woke him as a man is awakened out of sleep. This indicates that this vision concerns the arousal of consciousness. The angel then presented a golden candlestick to the prophet. This source of light contained a bowl for oil with seven lamps attached. The oil came from two olive trees which were connected to seven pipes. The candlestick likely represents the potential a person has for enlightenment, and the seven lamps represent the seven spiritual centers of man, storage places of enlightenment symbolized by light of different colors. It has been found by scientists that light, intelligent information, can reside in places in the body besides the brain. It has been found, for instance, that one may have brain cells in their stomach, the location of the body's interface with the third chakra.

The two olive trees in the fifth vision likely represent intercessory and governing functions. Olives, especially olive oil, have connotations of compassion and mercy. This is reinforced by what was said to Zerubbabel, "Not by might nor by power, but by my spirit, says the Lord." Zerubbabel was the governor, the one chosen to oversee the rebuilding of the temple after the return from Babylon. This vision then concerns a person having their seven chakras empowered through intercession. The vision indicates that light may be distributed throughout a person in many ways through this method.

The sixth vision was of a flying scroll. The fact that written information flew indicates that it was being disseminated. The scroll was ten cubits by twenty cubits, which is symbolic of its content. Twenty in Biblical mathematics represents redemption, and ten is symbolic of testimony and responsibility, which means that when a person utilizes redemption through grace they are required to made it manifest. [34] It was said that the scroll would be a curse on anyone who might steal or lie. This indicates that when a person functions through grace there is a negative reaction to any actions which do not faithfully and honestly witness to it.

The seventh vision was of a basket with a woman in it. She was said to represent wickedness, something which means perverse behavior. A woman represents the nurturing aspect in the human persona, and so here she must symbolize giving birth to perverse reactions to intercessory grace. A cover was placed over the basket and a lead weight kept the cover down, signifying the capture of the woman. Then the basket was said to have been sent to the plain of Shinar, which is in the land of Babylon, a country which has been seen to represent the ego drive in a person. This vision is then likely about the penalty for a person having access to divine grace and yet deciding not to live in it. The punishment for this is indicated to be an enforced journey into egotism, something which isolates a person from further benefits of grace so that they must personally bear all the penalties for erroneous actions.

The eighth and final vision was of four chariots coming from between two mountains of bronze. The horses were red, black, white and dappled. Commentators see bronze in the Bible as symbolic of strength and immutability.[35] Horses are conveyers of a given dynamic, and mountains likely symbolize political groups or belief systems. A fair assumption then is that the two mountains represent aspects of the Old Covenant, the one based on the law and the New Covenant, the one based on grace that fulfills the law. In scripture four is always symbolic of the earthly realm, and so the four chariots pulled by horses that have been presented before the Lord represent the conveyance of the two covenants throughout the earth. For a person this represents the manifestation of the law and grace in all aspects of their life. It is said then that the chariot with the black horses went to the north, and the spirit of the Lord would be at rest there. As has been seen, Babylon is the area to the north of the holy land, and that country represents the ego. Being at rest there likely means that modification of the ego has been sufficiently achieved. The white horse going to the west likely symbolizes dissemination of Christianity, as that system has been historically promulgated throughout the world in a westward manner. The dappled horses going to the south then likely symbolize the variety of religions in the area to the south of the holy land as they were the first to have belief systems such as Islam, and Buddhism. The red horse remaining in the holy land is consistent with the historical situation where that is the hot spot of the world, where Islam, Judaism, and Christianity are all centered. They all came initially through the father of faith, Abraham.

From this it is seen that principles of redemption through grace that fulfils the law are meant to be promulgated throughout the world in ways that are understandable to the various people groups which inhabit it. This is because everyone is ordained to function through grace, as all people have been created in the image of a gracious God. This idea is reinforced by a statement of Edgar Cayce that the reason for the many different religions in the world is because people have different needs, various deficiencies. He said that the world is like a vegetable garden and some people need the vitamins from carrots, some need lettuce, and others need sustenance from other vegetables. While this would account for the wide variety of religions in the world, the nature of Christianity is unique. The message of the cross supercedes religious differences, involving eventual crucifixion of the self, the entire self-concept. As the psychic, Rudolf Steiner, has said, "We cannot encounter the essential being of Christianity in other religions. It is not correct to place Christianity alongside other religious creeds." [36] This is the last of the eight visions in the second word, and all have presented the concept of a covenant where there is an intercessor, one who provides grace for all.

After the eight visions, there was a word to Zechariah that directed him to crown Joshua the High Priest, to make him the ruler. And then there were instructions to collect silver and gold from three exiles recently arrived from Babylon, the metal to be used to make a crown for Joshua, whose name means "savior". Since Babylon is symbolic of the ego, this means that at this state of progress a person has stopped functioning through the ego, and is instead using the grace of an intercessor. It was then decreed that Joshua the high priest, be called the Branch, the one growing and strong. This means that the High Priest, the intercessor, is destined to become increasingly stronger as a person accepts his functions. It was said that this intercessor was to build the temple, bear the royal honor, and sit on the throne. The temple, honor, and throne represent the status, glory, and authority of the intercessory priesthood, which is available to all.

The next segment of the word of the Lord to Zechariah came on the fourth day of the ninth month in the fourth year of the reign of Darius. As four is the number of the earth and nine is the number of the fruit of the spirit in Biblical mathematics, this part of the word must concern the fruit of the spirit in the world. In this word representatives from the town of Bethel asked the priests if the fasts they had done in the fifth and seventh months while in Babylon were effective. Babylon still symbolizes the ego and Bethel means "House of God", so the people from that town can be assumed to be destined to be godly. Five is the number of God's grace and seven is the number of completion, so this question is about the correct means of achieving godliness through grace. The answer Zechariah gave from the Lord implied that even when these rules of fasting were followed, they only yielded self-righteousness. The prophet said that true righteousness was instead to be achieved by helping a kindred soul. This was said to be through rendering true judgment and showing kindness and mercy. He said that one should not oppress the widow, the orphan, the alien, or the poor. This is a fast in which one knows of someone who has been left alone, deserted, alienated, or impoverished and a person is to treat them with compassion regardless of other considerations. In this way goodness is shown, as indicated by the statement that one should not devise evil against another on their bed. It was then said that a person should always have a positive attitude towards someone else, the implication being that this is what will be returned to him. This is said to supersede other attempts at fasting.

Then the word of the Lord came to Zechariah that he was jealous of Zion, he was protective of His holy mountain. A mountain in scripture represents a people group, a political entity, and the mountain of the Lord, Mount Zion, represents the nation of the chosen ones. Images were presented of old men and women being at rest and youngsters playing in the streets. This is where righteousness reigns in the land of the chosen people. It was said that Judah was previously a curse among the nations. This represents the situation where a person might have considered themselves one of the chosen ones, but behaved in a way that was self-righteous instead.

In the word it was said that Judah, the symbol of the holy center of the persona, would in the future be a blessing, something which would be accomplished through common assistance. This was characterized as fasts in the fourth, fifth, seventh, and tenth months, which were said to be times of joy and gladness. This is the adding of fasts in the fourth and tenth months to those in the fifth and seventh months. Four is the number of the earth and ten is the number of witness, and so qualities related to those numbers would be added to grace and completion. True righteousness was then to be accomplished by reliance on the grace which helps a person witness to it in the world. This is where all facets of a person might be pure and not just those that are ordained to be so. The result of this overflow of virtue from the holy center was then described.

It was indicated to be a refining process which would produce correction in nonproductive personal aspects. These psychic aspects are symbolized by geopolitical areas around the holy place of Judah. They are archetypes with psychic tendencies inherent in the names of Tyre, Sidon, Ashkelon, Gaza, and Ekron. For example, Tyre and Sidon symbolize trading for materiel prosperity and Gaza represents paganism. Those nations can then be looked upon as archetypes of different religious systems, those which emphasize specific aspects of goodness, but are not inherently pure. The preordained righteousness of the holy center, symbolized by Judah, was seen to influence the other areas, those which represent man-made religious systems. It would seem that what was initially proposed as the correct way to look at the Old Testament is now being defined. Righteousness then is to be seen not as the exercise of a religious system, but rather enlightenment which affects one's thoughts and behavior so they relate to their situation and others in the right manner.

Then it was said in the word that Zion would joyously receive her king who would come humbly on a donkey. When this state is reached, all sham, and religious posturing have been abolished, and a place has been created for a righteous ruler to be the only one. Having this humble messiah as ruler affects the self-concept and the holy center, symbolized here by Ephriam, and Jerusalem. It is said that he would cut off the chariot from Ephriam and the war-horse from Jerusalem. This represents the next step in the achievement of completion, which is the elimination of a false sense of prosperity and of self-righteousness. The holy center being in a state of peace, it is said that this condition would be extended to other areas as it is written that the sons of Zion would be aroused against the sons of Greece, the gentiles, to make them pure also. .

When the humble king comes into power in the holy place he will lead the crusade to achieve universal purity and peace. The result of this is ordained to be a consolidation of his power in all aspects of the psyche, symbolized by the strengthening of the House of Judah and the saving of the house of Joseph. The word said that then Egypt and Assyria would be brought back to Gilead and Lebanon, which are symbols of peace and security. Egypt has been seen to represent carnal flesh and Assyria is an archetype of ruthlessness, so this is a change in basic attitudes of a person. These are further steps in the development of the persona during the reign of the messiah in a place of holy power.

With the messiah ruling in the holy place and extending his rule, all is not complete, however, there is not yet shalom, or perfected peace. One is not perfected even though they are at peace and ruled by the universal intercessor. There is, of course, strengthening through him, as described in chapter eleven of the prophecy with images such as the cedars of Lebanon and the oaks of Bashan. However, the idea is presented that, with the help of constant intercession, a compassionate nature doesn't always follow. There is a quality of perversity in the universal psyche which will accept undeserved favor, and yet not always pass it along. This is symbolized by thirty pieces of silver, which is known as blood money, resources that are not sanctified.[37] In the psychic makeup of a person, this is the proclivity to avoid using the messiah, the constant intercessor, for universal good. Then an image of a worthless shepherd is presented, symbolizing the rejection of a humble universal leader through not sharing his benefits.

The next step is where the temporary rejection of the messiah is followed by Jerusalem and Judah being strong against all the nations that would come against them. This represents the overcoming of negative inclinations by a person when others would transgress against them. When this behavior is pursued, virtuous proclivities triumph in many areas. This can be seen where it is said that the feeblest among the holy ones in Jerusalem are triumphant against all outside foes, as David was against Goliath. Then, even when powerful outside foes are defeated, there is compassion for them. This scenario is likened to the day of the Lord, a preordained time of judgment against all impure inclinations, both historical and personal.

It is then said that the names of the idols would be cut off. When this occurs only absolute truth is the currency, and so now in addition to a lack of carnality, defects in meanings inherent in language are overcome. This is the promise of permanent residence at the level of the seventh chakra, where only the quiet of eternity prevails and all is pure. Then, however, there is the necessity for maintenance of this state without a ruler, as it is said that the shepherd would then be stricken and the sheep scattered. The sheep, those who represent pure personal qualities which have been developed thus far, then have to be sustained on their own. It is written that then two-thirds of the sheep will perish when they are scattered. Three is number of the triune nature of man, and so the meaning here is that when divine shepherding of the physical and relational aspects is taken away, only spiritual resources remain. There is always potential for carnality at the physical level and deception at the soul level, but when physical and relational power are taken away pure spiritual virtue is the only resource. This is the prophesized state here, functioning at the spiritual level completely.

The final physical conflict in the prophecy of Zechariah concerns Jerusalem, which is symbolic of the most holy center of the psyche. There is a word given that all nations will be gathered against the holy city and they will take it, loot it, and rape its women. This, in relation to a person, is where purity has been achieved in the holy center, but when the messianic ruler is removed, there is a universal assault on the person. This is the state where one has achieved purity of life, and yet is mercilessly assailed at every turn. This is represented in Zechariah by images of violence in the holy city. An apt image for this condition is what has been called, "The Dark Night of the Soul", a condition where a person is functioning in a pure manner and yet circumstances seem to conspire to destroy their very existence.

After this defeat of Jerusalem, the holy center, it is said that the Lord will return and fight against all foreign nations as on a day of battle. It is said that his feet will stand on the Mount of Olives, east of Jerusalem, and the Mount will be split in two from east to west. And the chosen ones will flee through the mountain valley as from an earthquake. The Mount of Olives represents common mercy and nurturing, and this is the way the chosen ones will survive in this final day of extreme distress. Finally it is said that the Lord, the God of all will then appear in the holy place and the chosen ones will be with him. In terms of the chakras, this is the prospect of permanent residence at the level of the seventh chakra for all personal attributes, a state of completed holiness. It is written that on that day there would be no cold or frost and it would be continual day. This is existence at a level where all dichotomies have been resolved and there is no perceived goodness or evil, but only wholeness and glory. Living waters will then flow out from Jerusalem, symbolizing unlimited resources for the pure persona. The Lord who created the heavens then will become king over all the earth, symbolizing purity becoming transcendent, not just in the center of the persona. This cosmic holy existence will be completely secure, symbolized by there being a plain from Geba to Rimnon, south of Jerusalem.

The final stage of history and personal development involves a plague against all peoples that might wage war against Jerusalem, the most holy center for the chosen ones. This is a defense against regression to a condition less than completed purity. There will be personal consciousness as in other states, but in a sanctified form. This is symbolized by a statement that all nations that warred against Jerusalem and survived would be allowed to worship the King, the Lord of Hosts. Then it is said that those nations that would not worship the Lord, as at the Feast of Tabernacles, would have plagues, symbolizing the ordained nature of completion of this highest state of existence

In this final stage, it is said that "Holy to the Lord" would be inscribed on the bells of the horses. In scripture, horses are conveyers of power, so the meaning here is that all activities in the cosmic personality would be entirely pure. It is also said that the cooking pots in the House of the Lord would be holy, symbolizing the imperishable nature of this state. Finally, it is said that there would be no traders in the house of the Lord of Hosts, symbolizing the lack of any possibility of apostasy from the final state of purity once it has been achieved.

This ends the book of the prophet whose name means, "Yahweh Remembers". It is a synopsis of growth to universal completion through grace. As such, it has parallels in the teachings of those individuals who have developed interpersonal psychology. Dr. Carl Jung was instrumental in this discipline with his description of individuation, or personal salvation. Dr. Jung described the process as one of progressing from functioning through the ego to a state of cosmic wholeness through consciousness of the Christ center in all people. This implies the perfecting of each individual as the world system is cleansed and perfected. From this it can be seen that principles in the Old Testament which are inviolate law may also be satisfied through grace, something to be seen in its entirety in the New Testament.

Malachi (My Messenger)   Dedication

The final book of the Old Testament, the final prophecy, and the last of the minor prophets, is Malachi. Scholars say this book was written after 516 B.C. E., which would have been after the temple in Jerusalem had been restored following exile in Babylon. In the context of personal development, the temple having been rebuilt symbolizes a place having been constructed in the psyche for an intercessor, the messiah. One must now only wait for him to appear. The previous book of Zechariah defined specific details about functioning through a gracious intercessor and now the messenger is saying that all one needs to do is wait for his functioning.

Malachi starts by saying that the Lord hated Esau, the carnal twin of Jacob. For a person this means that enlightenment involves more than willful seeking. Esau lived to satisfy his desires, while Jacob, the artificer, functioned in a more enlightened manner. Next it is said that polluted food has been placed on the altar and blind animals have been sacrificed. This represents the tendency of a person to rely on what is convenient in the world system instead of waiting for an intercessor. It is said that it would be better to close down the temple doors, to not even attempt to be righteous as the gentiles, who are just common people, worship better. This represents the principle that when a person tries to be righteous through his own will, all that is accomplished is self-righteousness, which is a pitiful state, worse than no attempt at righteousness at all.

In chapter two there is a condemnation of the priests of the time, those who go their own way and don't honor the name (authority) of the Lord Almighty. It is said that they will have a curse on them because of this. The ultimate cause of this condemnation was a failure to regard the principles of the law. It is said that the priests have not followed the Lord's covenant with Levi, the tribe which was designated to be those who would uphold the laws give by Moses. The implication of this is that the current priests forgot that none of the precepts of the Mosaic law can be circumvented. This has caused many to stumble. For a person this is the situation where they have acknowledged the intercessory grace of the messiah, but don't see him as one fulfilling the law rather there be superseding of it. This theme is expanded upon in a condemnation of the tribe of Judah. That tribe symbolizes prosperity and aggressiveness and is represented by a lion. This then is another condemnation of the personal tendency to fail to wait on the will of the Lord, instead of relying on personal power.

Proper behavior in Malachi is described as being receptive and thus eliminating attempts at purification through one's own will, something which symbolized here by flawed sacrifices. Chapter three of Malachi continues the theme of the reception of intercessory help where one is like a child waiting for a kind and powerful father.

Chapter four tells of the point where the final refinement of behavior takes place, where there is complete reliance on intercessory help. Then the tendency to try to perform righteous acts through one's own resources has been eliminated by the awareness of an infinitely greater power. It is said that when this would be a person's way, they should be conscious of Moses' laws – not through consciously following them, but seeing them as fulfilled through a messianic intercessor. This might be seen as permanent, continual residence at the level of the seventh chakra, where there are no conflicts. When this occurs one need only wait for the assistance of the intercessor, whose image has been perfected in them previously.

(Endnotes)

1 Psalm 105:37

2 Ibid, 13

3 The information in this section comes from "The Bible Through the Ages", Huber et al (The Readers Digest Association, 1989)

4 Cayce, Ellington et al. A Commentary on the Book of Revelation, (A.R.E. Press, 2000), 22

5 Ed F. Vallowe, Biblical Mathematics (Thg Olive Press, 1998), 80-84

6 The Complete Edgar Cayce Readings (A.R.E. Press, 1966), Reading 2528-2

7 The Chakra Handbook (Lotus Press, 2001), 63

8 Biblical Mathematics, 85-87

9 A commentary on the Book of Revelation, 72

10 The Complete Edgar Cayce Readings, Reading, R0254-025

11 J. Vernon McGee, Thru the Bible (Thomas Nelson, Inc, 1982)

12 Davidson, Stibbs, Kevan, et al. The New Bible Commentary (Wm. B. Eerdmans Publishing Compa nyt,1960), 564

13 Biblical Mathematics, 98-101

14 Dr. Carol S. Pearson, The Hero Within (Harper-Collins, 1986)

15 Ephesians 2:20

16 Mystical Christianity, John Sanford (Crossroad, 2000), 187

17 John Van Auken, Edgar Cayce on the Revelation (A.R.E. Press, 2000), 142

18 Thru the Bible

19 A Commentary on the Book of Revelation, 145

20 Nelson's Complete Book of Bible Charts and Maps, 212

21 Biblical Mathematics, 68-73

22 Thru The Bible, 525

23 The Hero Within, 219

24 Biblical Mathematics, 53-59

25 Ibid, 173-176

26 The New Bible Commentary, 720

27 Nelson's Complete Book of Bible Charts and Maps, 274-277

28 Biblical Mathematics

29 Ibid

30 Ibid

31 Ibid, 94-97

32 Nelson's Complete Book of Bible Charts and Maps, 274-277

33 Biblical Mathematics, 85-87

34 Ibid, 91-93

35 The New Bible Commentary, 735

36 Rudolph Steiner, Staying Connected (Anthroposophic Press, 1980), 49

37 Biblical Mathematics, 155-157

Appendix

The Meaning of numbers in Biblical Mathematics